Contents

Introduction   viii
The new exam format   viii
The evidence question   viii
    Sample evidence question answers   ix
The essay question   x
    Common essay question phrases   xi
    Essay subjects   xii
    Essay question planning and writing   xvii
    Sample essay question answers   xviii

Answers to evidence questions   Medieval realms: Britain 1066–1485   1
    1 The Norman Conquest   2
    2 The First Crusade, 1095–99   6
    3 Richard the Lionheart   7
    4 Archbishop Becket   9
    5 King John, 1199–1216   11
    6 The Black Death, 1348–50   12
    7 Henry V, 1413–22   14
    8 Women in medieval society   16
    9 Richard III, 1483–85   18

Answers to evidence questions   The making of the United Kingdom: 1485–1750   21
    10 Henry VII, 1485–1509   22
    11 Henry VIII and Anne Boleyn   24
    12 Henry VIII and the English Reformation, 1529–40   26
    13 Mary I and Lady Jane Grey   28
    14 Mary I   29
    15 Elizabeth I and Mary Stuart   33
    16 The causes of the English Civil War, 1629–42   35
    17 The execution of Charles I   37
    18 The Plague of London, 1665   38
    19 The Fire of London, 1666   40
    20 John Churchill, Duke of Marlborough   42
    21 The Jacobite Rebellion, 1745   44

Answers to evidence questions   Britain and Empire: 1750–1914   47
    22 The causes of the American War of Independence, 1763–76   48
    23 The Transport Revolution   50
    24 The Great Reform Bill, 1832   54
    25 The Chartists   56
    26 The Crimean War, 1854–56   58
    27 The Indian Mutiny, 1857   60
    28 Slavery   62
    29 Public health   64
    30 The Suffragettes   66

Answers to essay questions   1066–1914   69

Appendix   ISEB mark schemes   85

Introduction

History for Common Entrance 13+ Exam Practice Answers is addressed primarily to pupils who will be sitting the Common Entrance examination in history. However, teachers, tutors, parents, or indeed anyone else involved in the preparation for the examination, will also find it useful.

This book offers some worked examples, with advice and comment, of evidence and essay questions across the whole syllabus from 1066 to 1914, as presented in *History for Common Entrance 13+ Exam Practice Questions* by Gavin Hannah, ISBN 9781471809057 (2014). It is designed to be used by you working on your own or with guidance from others.

This book will be your partner helping you to succeed if you note, and then act on, what it says. But you must play your part as well. Success will be yours only through hard work and perseverance.

Revise thoroughly: Although narrative alone will not get you a top grade, you need to know the material thoroughly. Learn all your dates and facts. Only then will you be able to select what you need to do the best job.

Presentation and style: There is a lot of continuous writing in a history examination. Offer the examiner tidy exam answers. In reality, scripts have to be very bad indeed to be penalised for poor handwriting or spelling. Nonetheless, try to be as neat as you can. Try to write in a clear style. Say what you mean. Do not make your sentences too long or complicated.

Spelling: This is important. Do your best. If in doubt, make a short vocabulary list for each topic, or note your own problem words. Possible essay subjects are no longer suggested on the question paper, so you will have no guidance. Thus, be sure you can spell whatever words you might need, especially names of people and places you are writing about.

Handwriting: Make your script as clear and legible as you can. Remember that the person marking your exam has a lot to get through in a very short time. Your good handwriting will help and may even put you in favour with the examiner!

The new exam format

The examination paper will be 60 minutes long.
   You must attempt:
- **ONE** evidence question

- **ONE** essay question.

It is suggested that you spend **5** minutes reading and planning, then **20** minutes on the evidence question and **35** minutes on the essay question.

The evidence question (20 marks/20 minutes)

The evidence question will consist of two written sources (which may be contemporary, modern or a mix of both), and a third source that is pictorial. The question will always begin with the words: *'Using ALL the sources and your own knowledge ...'* and will ask you to consider a viewpoint derived from the sources.

   In this exercise you will be expected to demonstrate the following skills:
- comprehension

- comparison and corroboration by cross-referencing sources

- differentiation between first-hand evidence and hindsight

- deduction and interpretation

History
FOR COMMON ENTRANCE

13+

Exam Practice Answers

History
FOR COMMON ENTRANCE

13+

Exam
Practice
Answers

Gavin Hannah

GALORE PARK

AN HACHETTE UK COMPANY

Every effort has been made to trace all copyright holders, but if any have been inadvertently overlooked the publishers will be pleased to make the necessary arrangements at the first opportunity.

Although every effort has been made to ensure that website addresses are correct at time of going to press, Galore Park cannot be held responsible for the content of any website mentioned in this book. It is sometimes possible to find a relocated web page by typing in the address of the home page for a website in the URL window of your browser.

Hachette UK's policy is to use papers that are natural, renewable and recyclable products and made from wood grown in sustainable forests. The logging and manufacturing processes are expected to conform to the environmental regulations of the country of origin.

Orders: please contact Bookpoint Ltd, 130 Milton Park, Abingdon, Oxon OX14 4SB. Telephone: +44 (0)1235 827827. Lines are open 9.00a.m.–5.00p.m., Monday to Saturday, with a 24-hour message answering service. Visit our website at www.galorepark.co.uk for details of other revision guides for Common Entrance, examination papers and Galore Park publications.

Published by Galore Park Publishing Ltd
An Hachette UK company
Carmelite House, 50 Victoria Embankment, London EC4Y 0DZ
www.galorepark.co.uk

Text copyright © Gavin Hannah 2014

The right of Gavin Hannah to be identified as the author of this Work has been asserted by him in accordance with sections 77 and 78 of the Copyright, Designs and Patents Act 1988.

First edition published 2009
This edition:
Impression number   10 9 8 7 6
                     2019

Design and typography by DC Graphic Design Limited, Swanley Village, Kent
Printed and bound by CPI Group (UK) Ltd, Croydon, CR0 4YY

A catalogue record for this title is available from the British Library

ISBN: 978 1 471809 088

About the author

Educated at the University of Birmingham, St. John's College, Cambridge and Kellogg College, Oxford, Gavin Hannah taught history in an IAPS school for 30 years. He has also worked in independent senior schools, examined history at A Level and trained as an ISI Inspector. In 1988, he was elected a Fellow of the Society of Antiquaries. He lives in Oxford.

Acknowledgements

Many people have helped to produce this book. In particular, my thanks go to the following: at Galore Park; Tammy Poggo, my editor, for her enthusiasm in driving the project forward; to Chris Scrace, for speedy responses to my suggestions; to Lesley Staff for unravelling textual and source queries and Ruth Thomas for checking proofs. My pupils at Summer Fields endured much of the advice given in the introduction. Indeed, its final shape reflects their youthful experience and criticism. Finally, I thank my wife, Ann, for her tolerance and understanding while *History for Common Entrance: 13+ Exam Practice Answers* dominated the household.

Gavin Hannah
Oxford
January 2014

For Jackson, Milo and Orlando

- an understanding of provenance

- evaluation of the utility of the sources

- the ability to present an overview, supported by your own knowledge, which serves to place the sources into their historical context

When evaluating pieces of evidence with a specific question in mind, there are **four** main skills which you should note and seek to develop. These are: **comprehension**, **comparison**, the idea of the **utility** of a source in a given context, and the appropriate use of your **own knowledge**.

Comprehension means **understanding** the material. Without understanding, you cannot offer any meaningful responses. Regular practice with the appropriate sources will develop skills and techniques in this area. **Specialised vocabulary** for any particular period or topic should also be noted. For example, if you are learning about Thomas Becket, you should be familiar with the word 'martyr'. Likewise, when studying slavery you ought to know the meaning of the term 'Triangular Trade'.

Comparison means picking a clear theme or idea to compare. Remember that only two sources may be compared at any one time. You should get into the habit of cross-referencing sources with regard to one particular idea. You must consider the **differences** as well as the **similarities**. If you draw a rough table with rows and columns on a planning sheet, this will stop you trying to hold too many ideas in your head at the same time! Above all, be crystal clear about what it is you are trying to compare, otherwise your answer will be muddled.

Utility means **usefulness**. In evidence questions, it means how useful a particular source is **for a particular purpose**. You should always bear in mind the question which the examiners have set and assess the utility of the sources in relation to this. The **content** and **provenance** of a source are vital things to consider when judging the utility of a piece of evidence. If a source has good provenance, the chances are that it will be reliable. But be careful – reliability and usefulness are not the same thing. Even if reliable, a source may not necessarily be useful. It can only be useful if it is reliable **and** relevant to the particular question you are handling.

Your own knowledge will enable you to put the sources into their historical context, and as such is an important element when answering the evidence question. Each school year, the examination board sets two evidence question topics for each of the three historical periods. So you will be able to prepare the background history to your set topic.

All these skills can form part of a top-level answer if used properly. You should try to answer the question by making a judgement based on the direct use of the sources. Include valid statements on the reliability of the material, as well as relevant reference to your own background knowledge. Answers should be well structured with a clear beginning, middle and end.

Sample evidence question answers

This book contains model answers to the evidence questions.

- These are suggested answers only. The aim is that you should learn from these and then begin to assess your own work. It is often easy to see where you go wrong in a maths calculation or in a Latin sentence, but it is much harder to judge your own writing. However, frequent practice will help you to get to know what things you need to put into an answer to an evidence question to make it worthy of a top mark.

- Look at the model answers carefully and see how they fit in with the ISEB mark scheme for top answers (Level 3), which can be found at the back of this book. When you read them, focus on the structure and technique and not the opinions put forward.

- History answers are not 'right' or 'wrong' in the sense of those in a maths problem. Of course your dates and facts must be correct, but opinions vary. You can say anything you like as long as it is reasonable and sensible and you can back it up with evidence.

- Not everyone would agree with the opinions about the Norman Conquest, Mary I or the Transport Revolution expressed in these answers. There are as many possible answers as there are writers. But you must be sensible. Usually the subject you are discussing will itself give you guidance about what to say.

- When starting an evidence question, work out a 'thesis'. That means the line you are going to take. State your thesis at the start. Then argue for and against it using the sources and your own knowledge. Finally, provide a short conclusion which states your original thesis or opinion.

- All the answers in this book were written out in full in about 20 minutes, which is the normal time suggested for tackling such exercises. The answers might be considered too long by some people, but the top-level answers show what might be done and are something to which you should aspire.

- None of the answers is perfect, and there are plenty of alternative ways of earning the marks. This is of course both the beauty (and one of the difficulties) of history.

Finally, enjoy what you write: let your enthusiasm come through your script and impress your examiners!

The essay question (30 marks/35 minutes)

There will be ten essay titles from which you must select just **one**. Each question will be generic and open-ended. Up to 50 per cent of the marks could be awarded for good narrative. However, to produce a top-grade answer you should try to express opinions, formulate judgements and use your analytical skills to justify what you say.

Choose your essay question with care. Ensure that you are able to make a good and relevant essay from the title you choose and that you can relate your choice exactly to the question. For example, if you decide to write about the significance of the **consequences** of a war, make sure that the war you choose has plenty of consequences. Then, focus on them and their significance. Do not just tell the story of the war itself! Always ensure that you have enough material to write about. Can you say enough to answer the question thoroughly? Can it be relevant to the question?

Managing your time is important. Practise writing against the clock, particularly in the final run-up to the exams, and see how much you can write in a given amount of time. Having some idea of this will increase your confidence. If you qualify for extra time, make sure you follow the advice you are given on how to make the best use of it.

Make a **plan** to get a good structure. Include an **introduction** and a **conclusion** with reference to the essay title. Between these, there should be a series of **linked paragraphs**, each making a particular point and following on from the last in a logical way to form a clear framework of argument.

Narrative is important, indeed it is possible to score 50 per cent of the marks allowed for the essay for good narrative alone. But story telling on its own does not make a top-grade answer, so avoid this. Ensure that historical material is carefully used to underpin your arguments and to support your opinions. Comment on what you write and try to understand its importance in relation to the question. Do not make vague generalisations, and always have a piece of evidence to support what you say.

Be relevant, and use precisely selected knowledge. Keep a sense of focus. Produce a **question-led response**. Appreciate the difference between **Topic knowledge** and **Question knowledge**. Topic knowledge means everything you have been taught about a topic, such as medieval monasteries or Robert Walpole and his policies. Question knowledge means only the knowledge necessary to answer a particular question on that topic.

Above everything else, enjoy what you write and let that sparkle come through your script. After all, you have chosen to tackle that particular essay. Good luck!

Common essay question phrases

Essay question titles are broad and it is impossible to list every combination of words. However, you will find it useful to keep some of the following expressions in mind when studying historical material.

Look carefully at these phrases and become familiar with them. Think hard about what they actually mean. The purpose of this list is to generate in your mind a greater understanding of essay questions. Only when you fully understand the meaning of a question, will you be able to write a relevant and accurate answer. You could build up your own list of expressions as you meet more titles.

Two common, key question words are 'assess' and 'explain'.

Assess can mean to rate, to judge, to evaluate, to appraise, to give an opinion on the value of something, like giving it a mark out of ten.

Explain can mean to spell out, to say why, to say about something, to account for something.

Remember, you must interpret each of these words within the context of the particular question.

Some common essay expressions follow. These phrases do not make sense on their own, but they will always relate to an essay title from your particular period of study and to a particular subject (person, event, thing, place) that you are asked to write about.

● Explain the most important consequences of …

● Assess the importance of …

● Explain the significance of …

● Explain how successful … was

● Explain why … is remembered (could be an event, thing, place or a person)

● Explain the most important causes of …

● Explain the extent to which … was a threat to …

● Explain the reasons for the failure of …

● Explain the role of the leader in …

● Explain the importance of the work of …

● Explain the reasons for his or her fall from power.

● Assess the extent of his or her success.

● Assess the extent of his or her failure.

● Explain how … helped the lives of the people in …

● Explain the role of … in …

Essay subjects

Below are some top topic tips to help you choose your essay subject to match a particular question. It is important to choose carefully.

This is **not** a complete list. It is **vitally important** for you to be familiar with the official list of suggested study topics, which you can find in the History syllabus, available from the ISEB website: www.iseb.co.uk.

- Appendix II gives you suggested essay question topics for the period 1066–1485

- Appendix III gives you suggested essay question topics for the period 1485–1750

- Appendix IV gives you suggested essay question topics for the period 1750–1914

The suggested essay topics below are arranged under the five main study themes for each of the three time periods. You will most likely be concerned with only one time period.

Medieval realms: Britain 1066–1485

All the following essay titles relate to this period.

War and rebellion: war

Choose a war that you have studied and explain its most important causes.
Choose a war that you have studied and explain its consequences.
    Possible topics:
- The Norman Invasion of England

- The civil wars of Stephen and Matilda

- Henry II and his French wars

- Edward I and the conquest of Wales

- Edward I and his war in Scotland

- Edward II and Scotland

- Edward III and the Hundred Years' War

- Henry V and his French wars

- Henry VI, Joan of Arc and the end of the Hundred Years' War

- Lancastrians against Yorkists in the Wars of the Roses to 1485

War and rebellion: rebellion

Explain the causes of any rebellion from the period you have studied.
Explain the extent of the threat to the king of any one rebellion you have studied.
    Possible topics:
- The Peasants' Revolt (1381)

- Jack Cade's Rebellion (1450)

Events such as the Northern Rebellion (1069) and the activities of Hereward the Wake around Ely (1070–71) may not offer you enough to write about. Always consider whether there is enough material to produce a relevant, **question-led response.**

Government and Parliament

From the period you have studied, explain how any one political event affected the power of the king.
From the period you have studied, choose a time of political instability and assess its importance.

Possible topics:

- Feudal control under William I

- Henry II and the development of royal authority

- Baronial revolt under King John and Magna Carta (1199–1216)

- The development of Parliament under Henry III or Edward III

- Stephen and Matilda

- Edward II

- The reign of Henry VI

- Edward IV

Religion

Choose one important figure involved with religion and explain why he is remembered.

Assess the importance of the Church in the lives of ordinary people.

Possible topics:

- Key churchmen: Lanfranc, Anselm, Thomas Becket, William of Wykeham

- Cathedrals and parish churches after 1066

- The development of monasteries and nunneries after 1066

- The role of the Church in looking after the people

- The Crusades

- The struggle between the Crown and the Church

- John Wycliffe and the Lollards

Social history

Explain the importance of one historical event which changed the lives of people in the period you have studied.

Explain the significance of the changes to daily life in the period you have studied.

Possible topics:

- The Black Death (1348–50)

- Life in the medieval town

- Life in the medieval village

General topics and local history

Explain the role of women in the period you have studied.

Assess the importance of any one work of literature from the period you have studied.

Choose any important building that you know well and assess its importance to the local area and to history in general.

Possible topics:

- Women in medieval society

- Geoffrey Chaucer and *The Canterbury Tales*

- The study of a local cathedral or castle

- The study of a local museum or historical site

The making of the United Kingdom: 1485–1750
All the following essay titles relate to this period.

War and rebellion: war
Choose a war that you have studied and explain its most important causes.
Choose any military or naval commander and explain how his skills contributed to victory.
Possible topics:
- The Spanish Armada and the war with Spain
- The English Civil War (1642–49)
- The War of the Spanish Succession (1702–13)
- Career and achievements of Francis Drake
- The work of Oliver Cromwell
- John Churchill, Duke of Marlborough

War and rebellion: rebellion
Explain the causes of any rebellion from the period you have studied.
Assess the reasons for the failure of any rebellion in the period you have studied.
Possible topics:
- Pilgrimage of Grace (1536)
- The Monmouth Rebellion (1685)
- The 1745 Jacobite Rebellion

Events such as Kett's Rebellion (1549), the Prayer Book Rebellion (1549), Wyatt's Rebellion (1554), the Northern Rebellion (1569) or the Jacobite Rising (1715) may not offer so much to write about. Always consider whether there is enough material to produce a relevant, **question-led response**.

Government and Parliament
From the period you have studied, explain how any one political event affected the power of the king.
Explain the importance of the work of any one government minister.
Possible topics:
- Elizabeth and her parliaments
- The rise of parliament 1603–49
- The Glorious Revolution (1688)
- The Union with Scotland (1707)
- Thomas Wolsey; Thomas Cromwell
- William Cecil, Lord Burghley
- Edward Hyde, Earl of Clarendon (1660–67)
- Robert Walpole as prime minister

Religion
Choose one religious leader and explain the importance of his ideas.
Explain the importance of religious change in any period you have studied.
Possible topics:
- Thomas Cranmer
- Archbishop William Laud
- John Bunyan and his religious non-conformity
- The reformation of Henry VIII

- The religious reforms of Edward VI
- The religious policies of Mary Tudor
- The Elizabethan Church Settlement (1559)
- The rise of the Puritans under Elizabeth and the Stuarts

Social history

Explain the importance of one historical event which changed the lives of people in the period you have studied.
Explain the significance of the changes to daily rural life in the period you have studied.
　Possible topics:
- The Elizabethan Poor Law
- The Great Plague of London (1665)
- The Great Fire of London (1666)
- The expansion and development of the wool trade
- Enclosure for sheep in the sixteenth century
- Changes in urban and rural life during the first half of the eighteenth century
- Overseas trade and exploration

General topics and local history

Explain the importance of Britain's overseas territories in any period you have studied.
Assess the effects on England of the rise of any one foreign power.
Explain the importance of the work of any one scientist during the period you have studied.
　Possible topics:
- Exploration and settlement in North America and India
- French threats to Henry VIII under Francis I
- Spanish threats to England under Phillip II
- The rise of Louis XIV 1660–1713
- The scientific achievements of Isaac Newton
- The discoveries of William Harvey
- The role of women
- The importance of a local museum or historical site
- The role of artists and writers

Britain and Empire: 1750–1914

All the following essay titles relate to this period.

War and rebellion: war

Choose a war that you have studied and explain its most important causes.
Choose a war that you have studied and explain its consequences.
　Possible topics:
- The Seven Years' War (1756–63)
- The American War of Independence (1775–83)
- The Napoleonic Wars (1793–1815)
- The Crimean War (1854–56)
- The Boer War (1899–1902)

War and rebellion: rebellion

Explain the causes of any rebellion from the period you have studied.

Assess the reasons for the failure of a rebellion in any period you have studied.

Possible topics:
- The French Revolution

- The Indian Mutiny (1857)

Government and Parliament

From the period you have studied, explain how any one political event affected the lives of the people.

Explain the importance of the policies of any one government minister.

Possible topics:
- The Corn Laws (1815)

- Any one of the Reform Acts (1832, 1867, 1884)

- The Factory Acts

- The Repeal of the Corn Laws (1846)

- The work of prime ministers such as Lord Liverpool, Robert Peel, Gladstone, Disraeli and Herbert Asquith

- Great Power Rivalries (1871–1914)

Religion

Choose one important figure involved with religion and explain why he is remembered.

Assess the importance of any one major challenge to the Church of England.

Possible topics:
- Cardinal Newman

- Samuel Wilberforce

- The Oxford Movement

- The growth of Methodism

- Roman Catholicism and the Catholic Relief (Emancipation) Act (1829)

Social and economic history

Explain the importance of any major historical event which changed the lives of people in the period you have studied.

Explain the significance of Britain's overseas trade in the period you have studied.

Possible topics:
- The Agrarian Revolution

- The Industrial Revolution

- The Transport Revolution

- The development of law and order through the police force

- The growth of working class movements

- The development of the British Empire in India

- Colonisation and the scramble for Africa

General topics and local history

Choose any one important event in the period you have studied and explain why it should be remembered.

Assess the importance of the achievements of any person in the field of medicine, science, art or literature.

Possible topics:
- The Great Exhibition (1851)
- The Irish Potato Famine (1845–51)
- The unification of Germany (1871)
- The role of women
- The importance of visiting a local museum
- The importance of visiting a historical site either at home or abroad

Numerous individuals such as:
- Florence Nightingale
- Charles Darwin
- Joseph Lister
- Sir John Millais
- John Constable
- Charles Dickens
- Thomas Hardy
- George Eliot

Essay question planning and writing

The aim here is for you to think about the whole process of writing an essay 'from brain to paper'. Written out in full, this might look complicated. Your brain, however, will deal with all this in seconds!

Example essay title:
Explain the consequences of any war you have studied.

Steps

1 **Choose your war.** What have you been taught? Have you revised it? Does your choice fit the question? Can you write relevantly? Can you write enough?

2 **Think.** What is the essay about? It is about the **consequences** of your chosen war so you must focus on these. It is **not** about the war itself. You must **not** write a narrative of the war.

3 What **are** the consequences of your chosen war?

4 You will **plan** them. You will jot them down in 'brain order' (as you think of them) then put them into a better order by placing a number against each item. You can change this as you think through the sequence simply by changing the numbers. You can then write them as your essay in the final number order, not in the order they first came out of your head. In history there is often no 'correct' order as such, but you must remember that there is usually a sensible or logical arrangement for the material.

5 **How many consequences** have you got? This will help with the timing. You have **35** minutes at the most to complete all your planning and to write the essay.

6 **Beginning your essay.** Write a **short introduction**. This may be a few lines of narrative to set the scene. This will put your following answer into context. Such writing also suggests to the examiners that you know your stuff and generates initial confidence in what you write.

7 The **main body of your essay** concerns the consequences and results of the war. Write each consequence as a new paragraph. You must comment on the **significance** of each factor you mention. This means saying something about why it was important for British history at the time, what effects it had or what changes it produced, all closely linked to the question. This is your analysis. It shows that you understand what you are writing about.

8 End with a **strong conclusion** which relates to the title and tries to say something general and sensible about what you have written in relation to the question. It may even place the particular question topic into a wider historical context.

Sample essay question answers

This book contains model answers to a selection of essay questions.

- These are suggested answers only. The aim is that you should learn from these and then begin to assess your own work.

- Look at the model answers carefully and see how they fit in with the ISEB mark scheme for top answers (Level 3), which can be found at the back of this book. When you read them, focus on the structure and technique and not the opinions put forward.

- History essay answers are not 'right' or 'wrong'. Your dates and facts must be correct, but opinions may vary.

- Each of the answers was written out by hand in about **35** minutes, which is the normal time suggested for the examination, **including planning.**

- None of the essays is perfect. Indeed there are plenty of alternative ways of earning the marks. You may not agree with some of the views expressed, but focus on the structure, or in some cases, lack of it!

ANSWERS TO EVIDENCE QUESTIONS
MEDIEVAL REALMS: BRITAIN 1066–1485

1 The Norman Conquest

Here are three attempts to answer this question, which reflect the different standards of answer as described in the ISEB mark scheme (see page 86). Pay particular attention to those at **Level 3**. This is the standard you are aiming for: the others are there to show you what **not** to do!

→ Question

Using **ALL** the sources and your own knowledge, how true is it to say that the Battle of Hastings completed the Norman Conquest of England?

Level 3 answer

In 1066, William the Conqueror won a great victory at the Battle of Hastings. But did the battle complete his conquest of England? A case may be made suggesting that Hastings was not the end of the Norman Conquest, but only the start.

Source C shows William leading his knights to victory. The English are beaten. But the source does not offer much correct information. It is based on the imagination of a nineteenth-century artist. It is useful for giving an impression of what the battle may have been like, but it is not accurate. Nonetheless, the event it illustrates did take place. After a long march from victory in the north, at Stamford Bridge, Harold and his army were defeated at Hastings and the English were conquered.

Source A adds to this idea of the conquest of England at Hastings. It states that the English lost 'a great part of their army', that Harold and his brothers were killed and that the rest ran away into the forests. But this material needs to be handled with care. William of Poitiers was biased. As a chaplain to the Conqueror, he was a Norman supporter. He further shows this by describing the English as 'rebels'. He was not even at the battle! However, he wrote about an important historical event where the English lost.

On the other hand, perhaps Hastings represented just the beginning of the Norman Conquest. After 1066, William did much to extend Norman power. He constructed castles, starting with the quickly built wooden forts of the motte-and-bailey type. These were followed by the great stone keeps, such as those at the White Tower at the Tower of London, completed by 1100, or those at Castle Hedingham and Rochester.

Source B talks about castle building, as well as the tightening up of the feudal system. William gave land to his tenants-in-chief who passed land to their own knights. Estates were held in return for military service. Men swore oaths of homage to their lords and to the king. All this helped the Normans to control England.

Source B, from a modern historian, should be accurate and reliable. The writer will have done careful research to try to find out the truth about the past. The evidence here suggests that much of the Norman Conquest of England gradually took place after 1066.

The Norman Conquest was also extended through a reorganisation of the Church, as mentioned in **Source B**. An extensive building programme led to many new cathedrals, like that at Norwich, in the years after 1096. Many parish churches were also rebuilt and monasteries were more strictly controlled. The production of *Domesday Book* (1086) also gave the Norman kings more power. **Source B** speaks of this 'great survey' which listed what land each tenant had, as well as land use, acreages and land value. The Norman conquerors now knew what they owned.

A new language – Norman French – was introduced for the new ruling classes. Trade developed through the closer links with Normandy, but it was mainly Frenchmen who benefited.

Rebellions by the English, such as those by Hereward the Wake in the Fens and the Northern Uprising of 1069, were savagely crushed by William. This also reinforced the idea of Norman domination. Royal judges toured the country administering the king's laws. All these factors meant that England increasingly felt the weight of harsh Norman authority.

To sum up, it does not seem true to say that the Battle of Hastings completed the Norman Conquest of England; 1066 was more a beginning than an end.

Comments related to mark scheme
- Well-structured answer: introduction; arguments for the question statement; arguments against the question statement; strong and clear conclusion where a judgement is reached in relation to the question statement.

- Clear statement of a thesis which is then defended.

- This is an analytical answer clearly related to the question. The first paragraphs argue for the question statement. There is a change of direction with the phrase, 'On the other hand …' (This is a very useful phrase.)

- The arguments are based on valid comments made on the content of the sources.

- There are valid statements concerning the reliability and provenance of the sources.

- There is some cross-referencing of sources.

- Own knowledge is clearly and appropriately related to the question.

- The final opinion is based on the direct use of both sources and own knowledge.

Level 2 answer

Sources A and **C** show that the Battle of Hastings did complete the Norman Conquest of England. In **Source C** we can see William leading his Norman knights against the English who look as though they are being beaten. This source also says that the battleground was stained with the blood of the English nobility.

William of Poitiers also describes how England was conquered in this battle. He says that the English lost most of their army and that the English king and his two brothers were killed. This was bad for England as they were very important men. After the battle, William the Conqueror was crowned king of England in Westminster Abbey on Christmas Day 1066.

Source A is a useful account of the battle. It gives lots of little details such as how the English bodies were left in the forest, while other Englishmen were trampled under the hooves of the Norman horses. All this shows that the Normans beat England at Hastings.

William of Poitiers was a Norman so he said nice things about the Normans. He was biased to William's side. He was not even at the battle though he says that Duke William did brave things and 'spared none who came against him'.

The modern writer of **Source B** just describes what the Normans did after the battle. William's lords were given estates and the feudal system was made better.

The Normans were also great castle builders and this helped them to control the English. Domesday Book was important because it showed William how much land he had and what it was used for and how many animals and villagers there were.

Castles and monasteries were made better and many cathedrals were started, like the one at Norwich. The White Tower was also built in London. This meant that William could send his prisoners there and keep the English in control after he had won at Hastings.

Comments related to mark scheme

● Some links are made between the sources, own knowledge and the question.

● There is some selection of evidence, both from the sources and from own knowledge to show that the Normans acquired great power over England, as in the opening paragraph. But, overall, comments in relation to the question are underdeveloped.

● Much of the information in the sources is recounted without any comment, for example, much more could have been made of the fact that Harold and his brothers were killed.

● The piece lacks planning and structure.

● There is no clear, final judgement either for or against the question statement.

● On the positive side, there is a hint of cross-referencing of the sources in relation to Sources A and C.

● There is also some attempt, although underdeveloped, to assess the reliability and utility of Source A. This should secure a sound Level 2 grade, but there is nothing concerning the provenance of Sources B and C.

● There is some relevant background knowledge, such as that concerning William's coronation and the content of Domesday Book, but it is insufficiently developed in relation to the question.

Level 1 answer

The picture in **Source C** shows the Battle of Hastings and we can see that the Normans are winning. It was a fierce battle and the ground was stained with blood. King Harold was hit in the eye with an arrow and died. The Normans are riding horses. But the English are fighting on foot so they could be beaten more easily.

In **Source A**, William of Poitiers tells the story of the battle. He says that the English knew that they could not hold out longer and that most of their men were dead. King Harold and his brothers died.

Duke William was a hero. He fought well for the Normans. The English were chased into the forest. A lot of them were killed. Some English soldiers died because they fell under Norman horses. The Normans chased the English off the battlefield. The English lost. The Normans had won a 'famous victory'.

William then had to give rewards to his barons as it says in **Source B**. He did this by giving them land taken from dead Saxons. **Source B** tells us a lot of things. William's men sometimes built castles. After the battle, William's lords had to give him a certain number of knights when he told them to. This made armies for William whenever he wanted. This was the feudal system which the Normans had in England.

Domesday Book was an important book. It told William lots of things about England. The Normans made a new language for England. This was called Norman French and was spoken by the upper classes to separate them from the peasants. The Church was strict. Lots of bishops came from France to rule over England. There were also abbots who came.

Comments related to mark scheme

● The comments are mainly descriptive of the sources with material simply reported back to the reader with no attempt to assess the significance of what is said.

● Comments are largely undeveloped.

● No attempt to relate the source material directly to the question.

● No reference to the question at all! Why indeed was the piece written? (Other than the need to produce something in the exam!)

● No specific arguments for or against the question statement.

● No conclusion regarding the truth or otherwise of the question statement.

● No attempt to compare the sources through cross-referencing.

● No reference to the provenance or reliability of the sources.

● Some little reference to own knowledge, though this is undeveloped.

● There is no overall structure, other than that naturally occurring from a description of each source in turn.

● Overall, this is a generalised answer although it demonstrates some understanding of the source material. However, there is no real attempt to use the evidence and own knowledge to produce a relevant answer to the question.

2 The First Crusade, 1095–99

→ Question

Using **ALL** the sources and your own knowledge, is it true to say that the First Crusade achieved all its aims?

Answer

It may be argued that the First Crusade achieved some of its aims in the short term, but that in the longer term it did not manage all it set out to do.

One of the major aims of the crusade was to recapture Jerusalem for the Christians. This was achieved in July 1099 as shown by the sources.

Sources A and **B** describe the attack with the scaling ladders and with armed soldiers rampaging through the streets and slaughtering all in sight without mercy. **Source C** illustrates the event in great detail.

The evidence from **Source A**, a modern book, ought to be accurate and reliable as it is a textbook. The author would have researched to try to find the truth about the event. **Source B**, even though written by a person nearer to the time of the fall of the city, is less reliable. William of Tyre was not there and he wrote with hindsight. His account is also biased, as he is writing from the side of the Christians.

The picture in **Source C**, although useful for giving an impression of what might have happened, is hardly accurate in its detail. The image comes from the imagination of a nineteenth-century artist. Nonetheless, all the sources agree on the fact that the city was taken.

Further evidence of the early success of the First Crusade is the fact that before the fall of Jerusalem the crusaders had captured the cities of Nicaea and Antioch. After 1099, the crusaders set up the Crusader States to try to hold the area for Christianity.

However, success was limited. There was constant Muslim unrest within the Crusader States and a thin Christian army of occupation struggled to keep control.

The Muslims and Jews could hardly be expected to be kind to Christians after the cruelty they endured in the fall of Jerusalem as shown in the sources. There was also intense hatred of the Turks by the Christians as mentioned in **Source B**. This situation was hardly going to lead to all the peoples peacefully living together.

That the First Crusade failed in the long term is also shown by the fact that a series of further crusades had to take place, such as the Third Crusade (1187 onwards) and the Fourth Crusade (1202–04), to try to recapture the Holy Land for the Christians. There was even a crusade as late as 1383, encouraged by the Bishop of Norwich.

Thus, it may be said that the First Crusade had some short-term successes, but that it failed in the longer term. Because of this fact, it is not true to say that all its aims were achieved.

3 Richard the Lionheart

→ Question

Using **ALL** the sources and your own knowledge, is it true to say that Richard the Lionheart merely used England as a bank from which to take money to pay for all his foreign adventures?

Answer

It may be argued that Richard I's great love of expensive foreign adventures led him to use England as a bank to pay for them.

Richard was a great warrior who was mainly interested in fighting. His most famous exploits are those connected with the Third Crusade (1187–92) but also, in his later years, he fought against Philip II, king of France. These latter campaigns were perhaps more necessary (if expensive), because as king of England, Richard was also Duke of Normandy and Aquitaine, as well as Count of Anjou and Maine. This made conflict with France very likely and Richard had to fight to maintain England's interests despite the cost.

However, Richard clearly favoured fighting abroad. **Source A** speaks of his military exploits and sums him up as 'a fearless warrior' and a 'glorious crusader'. This source, from a modern textbook, should be reliable. The author will have studied carefully in order to try to present a true picture of events.

This idea of Richard as a great fighter enjoying his expensive foreign adventures is reflected again in **Source B**. Here, we note that Richard cannot wait to get away quickly enough on Crusade after he had just become king, so that he could 'avenge the wrongs of Christ'. This is a contemporary source, written close to the events it describes. The writer has no reason to be biased. It ought to be reliable, but nonetheless it should be interpreted with care.

Source C further supports **Sources A** and **B** in suggesting Richard's love of foreign adventures. Here, Richard is seen on the Third Crusade. This is an action picture of the king fearlessly striking down his enemies. It was painted only in modern times and does not reflect reality, despite giving a vivid impression of how Richard might have looked in battle, enjoying one of his adventures.

Even though Richard remained in England for only six months of his reign, he did not neglect his government. He placed high officials in charge of the administration while he was away, so that the whole system of government remained in place. Indeed, the role of certain officials grew more important and there was an increase in the number of government records which were produced. As it says in **Source A**, Richard had 'a care for the safety of his kingdom'. He did not totally neglect it. This agrees with **Source B** from which we learn that Richard placed people in key positions as regents, hoping to keep England in order while he was away.

Despite this, Richard clearly liked fighting abroad above all else, as all the sources show. Such adventures were expensive; Richard squeezed England for lots of money. He taxed the Church heavily. He sold government jobs. He sold land. He forced officials to pay large sums of money to keep their places in government. It is said that Richard even once claimed that he would sell London if he could find a buyer.

Richard loved adventure and military glory. He liked being away from England (despite being born in Oxford) where he said it always rained! When not on campaign, he spent most of his time in Aquitaine.

In conclusion, both from history in general and from these sources in particular, the evidence suggests that owing to his passionate love of foreign military exploits and because of the wealth available in England, Richard I did indeed use his kingdom like a bank to provide the money for all his foreign adventures.

Notes: _____

_____

_____

_____

_____

_____

_____

_____

_____

_____

_____

_____

Archbishop Becket

→ Question

Using **ALL** the sources and your own knowledge, do you think that Thomas Becket caused his own death?

Answer

The evidence from all these sources, as well as the background circumstances, strongly suggests that Becket's death in 1170 was his own fault. Becket had full control of many of the factors which led to his martyrdom, but did nothing to stop them.

But what may be said against this view? There are perhaps two main things which Becket could not influence. The first was Henry II's temper. Driven to distraction by Becket's stubborn attitude, the king, in France, is supposed to have shouted out, 'Will no one rid me of this turbulent priest?' Becket could not stop this.

Secondly, on hearing the king, the four knights, as named in **Source C**, journeyed to England and violently murdered Becket at Canterbury on 29 December. Again, Becket could not prevent their intentions.

However, there is much to suggest that Becket brought death upon himself. **Source A** mentions that he made no attempt to escape from the knights. According to this author, there were various doors and ways which were open to him and he could 'easily have saved himself by escape'. Instead, he ordered the monks not to bolt the door and offered himself to death. This source further states, 'the prospect of being a martyr was not unwelcome to him'.

Source A, from a modern historian, will have been carefully researched to try to offer an accurate account. This is a reliable and useful source. It strongly supports the notion of Becket's self sacrifice.

The same idea is reflected in **Sources B** and **C**. Becket is said to be 'ready to suffer' and to offer himself 'as a living sacrifice' (**B**). The illustration in **C** shows Becket at the altar making no attempt to save himself.

Source B is an eyewitness account and ought to be reliable and accurate. However, Grim, as a clerk and biographer of Becket, may have favoured him. His story may be biased, exaggerating Becket's bravery. **Source B** must be used with care.

Source C, too, requires careful handling. It was probably produced by the Church which would want to show Becket in a good way. It was made long after the event it shows when the Becket story had passed into folklore. Despite all this, all the sources still suggest that Becket was responsible for his own martyrdom.

The historical events leading to his death also support this view. Becket constantly irritated Henry II. After 1162, the archbishop championed the rights of the Church, wanting clerks in Church courts as opposed to royal courts. He refused to accept any restrictions on the Church in the Constitutions of Clarendon (1164). From his exile in France, Becket opposed the coronation of Henry's son, Prince Henry, by Roger, Archbishop of York. He even appealed to the Pope over this matter. Becket, by his constant stubbornness, increased the tension between himself and Henry II. Finally, the king snapped and Becket's death was the result.

To sum up, the evidence that Becket caused his own death would seem to be overwhelming. It is indeed true to say that Thomas Becket's death was his own fault.

Notes:

5 King John, 1199–1216

→ Question

Using **ALL** the sources and your own knowledge, how far is it true to say that John was a bad king?

Answer

King John had a troubled reign and the majority of the evidence suggests that he was a bad king.

Source B argues that John was a hardworking, energetic king and a good administrator and judge. This source, as the work of a modern historian, ought to be accurate and reliable. The author would have carried out thorough research in an attempt to get at the truth about the past. However, all this does not necessarily make John good.

There is no doubt that John was unfortunate in facing some powerful opponents. Philip II of France was a strong king, fully committed to reducing England's power on the Continent. Innocent III, one of the greatest medieval popes, allowed nothing and no one to interfere with the power of the Church.

However, judged by the standards of the age, John was seen as a bad king. A good king was supposed to be successful in war and John failed. He lost Normandy in 1204 and was defeated again at Bouvines (1214), which served to confirm French power. As a result, John's barons were angry.

A good medieval king was supposed to protect and maintain the rights of the Church. In this John failed. He abused his power, taxing the Church and interfering with its rights and privileges. Innocent III grew angry. England was placed under an Interdict in 1209 and surrendered as a Papal Fief in 1213. Again, John's barons were furious.

John also had a bad character. He is supposed to have murdered his nephew, Arthur, in the interests of his own power. **Source A** deals with this event. However, this was produced by a churchman who would have hated John. It is a biased source as we see from both its content and language. John was described as a tyrant 'possessed by the devil'. It says that he killed Arthur 'with his own hand', which is unlikely.

But although this evidence is unreliable, it nonetheless refers to a true event when Arthur was secretly deposed. This is hardly the action of a good king.

To John's failures in war and with the Pope must be added his abuse of feudal power. John raised unjust taxes and took illegal scutage. He forced widows to marry and charged heavy-handed reliefs. John also abused the Law, selling justice to some while denying fair trials to others. Again, these are the actions of a bad king.

From all this came the signing of Magna Carta as illustrated in **Source C**. The exact details of this nineteenth-century picture are hardly true, but the event it depicts did happen. The very fact that it happened suggests that John was bad. Much of what the Charter tried to put right with feudal customs, the Church and the Law, also tells us what John had been doing wrong and just how bad a king he was.

Like **Source A**, **Source C** indirectly shows us that John was a bad king. **Source B** refers to John as a bad king and the general events of history add truth to this view.

6 The Black Death, 1348–50

→ Question

Using **ALL** the sources and your own knowledge, do you agree that the effects of the plague were more than just social?

Answer

The evidence from all the sources and the general historical background suggest that it is correct to agree with the question statement that the effects of the plague in 1348 were far more than social.

Social effects remain important nonetheless. **Source C** shows some effects of the plague in a village. As a modern drawing, it cannot be a true reflection of a real village burial. However, the source is accurate to the extent that it represents what actually occurred.

About one-third of the English population died. In some places, whole villages were wiped out and became deserted. This idea of a decreasing population is supported by **Source B**, which says that the population shrank. **Source B** should be accurate and reliable, being the work of a modern historian who will have studied carefully in an attempt to present the truth.

One further social consequence of the plague was increasing geographical mobility among the peasantry as villeins moved from one village to another seeking better wages. Other peasants tried to increase their social rank. Seeing wages rising, they tried to change their status from tenants doing labour services to that of wage-earning freemen paying rent. In such a way they could make more money.

There were many economic effects of the plague. **Source B** mentions that wages increased as survivors could charge more for their work. Indeed, after 1348 there was a shortage of workers and the government took political action to ensure a cheap supply of labour by capping wage rates at pre-plague levels, through an Ordnance of 1349 and the Statute of Labourers (1351), both unpopular with peasants.

In the longer term, there were troubles with violence against lords, especially Church landlords and monasteries. The Peasants' Revolt of 1381 was the eventual result of much of this. It may be argued that this event was a long-term effect of the plague and of the government's response to it.

Agricultural production fell as land went uncultivated. More fields were turned from arable to pastoral farming, as this required less labour.

Towns were affected, too. In economic terms, depopulation led to a reduction of trade and output in the little craft industries. It was several decades before general commerce was back to pre-plague levels.

No one understood the causes of the plague. The doctors were confused. Many churchmen saw the 1348 visitation as a punishment by God for the sins of the world. This belief is well illustrated in **Source A** as it says, God sent 'a general shower of death throughout the kingdom' to punish all the 'wanton buffoonery' of the age.

This source, written by a churchman, is obviously biased. We now know it to be untrue as we understand the real causes of the disease. Nonetheless, it remains useful, illustrating as it does a contemporary view. Fearing death, many would have turned to the Church for help.

In conclusion, it may be agreed that the consequences of the plague were far more than social. Economic, political and religious effects, in the long and short term, were also important results of this fourteenth-century disaster.

Notes: _____

_____

_____

_____

_____

_____

_____

_____

_____

_____

_____

_____

Henry V, 1413–22

→ Question

Using **ALL** the sources and your own knowledge, do you agree that Henry's victory at Agincourt actually achieved very little?

Answer

It is not true to say that Henry V's victory at Agincourt achieved very little. There were considerable political and military gains, but the latter were mainly in the short term.

After Agincourt, the war went well for England, so that by 1420 Charles VI was desperate to make peace. By the Treaty of Troyes, Henry V controlled half of France and it was agreed that he should take over as king on the death of Charles VI. These were hardly little gains, but they only lasted a short time.

As **Source A** states, ultimate English victory was only 'a daydream', and, after Agincourt, Henry V led 'his country into a war which could never be won'. **Source A**, as the work of a modern historian, should be reliable and accurate, based on careful research and study. It certainly agrees with what happened in the years after 1415.

In 1429, the English army was defeated by Joan of Arc at the Siege of Orléans. Then the French, with renewed vigour, slowly regained much of their lost territory. The Duke of Burgundy, a former ally of the English, went over to the French side in 1435. This represented a major blow to English military fortunes. By 1453, the English had lost the whole of France apart from Calais and the French were masters in their own country. Thus the long-term results of Agincourt seemed slight.

On the other hand, there were some lasting military results. The Battle of Agincourt saw the death of many top French knights, which weakened France for a long time. The battle also demonstrated how an attack by fully armoured knights could be defeated by the skills of the English longbowmen.

Source B describes this in great detail. The French were 'disabled and wounded by the arrows'. The attacking knights, on the flanks of the battle-line, came to grief on the stakes placed in front of the archers, as well as by the press of their own men. This tactic was a great achievement and certainly not a waste from the English point of view.

There was also much bloody hand-to-hand fighting, as the English closed in to defeat dismounted French knights. Much of this is shown in **Source C**. This evidence needs to be used with care. Such an illustration is not realistic, but it illustrates a true idea. To the right of the picture, we see dead and dying Frenchmen with some of their banners on the ground. Clearly, Henry V's men are winning.

Source B, on the other hand, although French, would seem to be balanced and reliable in describing the disasters happening to the knights. It is also an eyewitness account. De Wavrin actually saw the battle.

Henry's victory at Agincourt had many political results. The fortunes of the monarchy, as **Source A** says, had been restored and Henry returned to England in triumph. This triumph has continued, helped by authors such as Shakespeare. In his play *Henry V*, the king is regarded as an action-man hero, described as a glorious 'star of England'.

Henry V's victory at Agincourt may have brought relatively little long-term military benefit, but much else was won besides victory, as England's military reputation was increased. Thus it is certainly not true to say that victory at Agincourt achieved 'very little'.

Notes: _____

_____

_____

_____

_____

_____

_____

_____

_____

_____

_____

_____

Women in medieval society

→ **Question**

....

Using **ALL** the sources and your own knowledge, how far do you agree that medieval women were unimportant?

Answer

Despite some evidence to the contrary, it is not correct to argue that women were unimportant in medieval life.

There were, however, some restrictions on women. Women were not allowed to enter parliament or professions such as medicine. In some ways they could indeed be seen as second-class citizens. As **Source A** mentions, after the Norman Conquest women lost status and the main medieval attitude followed that of the Church, which saw women as inferior to men. **Source A** states that women had to obey first their fathers and then their husbands. Only towards the end of their lives could there be a greater sense of freedom.

Source A, written by a modern historian, should be accurate and reliable. The author should have tried to find out the truth. As such, **Source A** is useful for assessing the place of women in medieval times.

However, there is much evidence to contradict this view and to suggest that women of all classes had an important part to play in life. The wives of noblemen often had a key role in looking after estates and castles while their lords were away, as outlined in **Source B**. **Source B** lists some of the skills such women ought to have. They had to manage accounts and understand the basics of agriculture such as when to sow seed, in order to direct their peasants properly. Hiring labourers and making them work hard meant the need for good judgement of character as well as management skills.

As a sort of instruction book, **Source B** perhaps suggests what the ideal noblewoman should be like. Nonetheless, it is probably accurate and reliable. It offers a view of how contemporaries saw the duties of such women. Thus it is a useful source for assessing the importance of women.

Many upper-class women were rich heiresses. They played a key part in the marriage market, helping to bind old families together and to create new networks. Lady Margaret Beaufort, daughter of the Duke of Somerset, married four times. From her second husband, Edmund Tudor, sprang Henry, the future King Henry VII. Margaret's role was important indeed!

Many middle-class women played their part by keeping efficient households. Sometimes detailed books were written to guide them in this, like that for the ménagier's wife in fourteenth-century Paris. Some women served the Church in nunneries, although many of these like Chaucer's Madame Eglentyne had a fairly easy life!

Source C shows lower-class women spinning and carding wool. As the wool trade was an important part of England's economy, generating much wealth, we can see that women's contribution was considerable.

Source C is one of many illustrations found around the text of old documents. There is no reason to suppose they are unreliable. These little drawings, like **Source C**, often just reflect the everyday things of life. Thus this is a useful and important source for showing us what women did.

The *Luttrell Psalter* shows women reaping at harvest time. There are other pictures of women carrying sacks of corn to a mill. It is clear from these that women played a notable part in agriculture.

To sum up, despite the comments in **Source A**, there is plenty of evidence suggesting that women of all classes played an important role in medieval life. Despite the restrictions on their activities, women were a key part of the community.

Notes: _____

_____

_____

_____

_____

_____

_____

_____

_____

_____

_____

_____

_____

9 Richard III, 1483–85

→ Question

Using **ALL** the sources and your own knowledge, should Richard III be seen as anything more than a cruel and ruthless usurper?

Answer

There is much argument surrounding the reign of Richard III (1483–85) and it is almost impossible to reach a final judgement on whether or not this king was a cruel and ruthless usurper.

The evidence that Richard murdered his way to the throne is covered in mystery and much is unreliable. **Source A** is a good example of this. It says that Richard had 'nothing but cruel and savage things in mind' and that James Tyrell murdered Edward IV's sons, the horror of which was 'nearly unheard-of within human memory'. This is clearly an exaggeration. This source is biased. Polydore Vergil published his account well after the supposed murder of the Princes by Richard. Its bias was probably shaped by Henry VII as a part of the Tudor propaganda to strengthen their relatively weak claims to the throne.

Source C agrees with **Source A**. It offers an illustration of Richard's cruelty in usurping the throne. But this is an imaginary nineteenth-century picture. The details are inaccurate, thus the source is unreliable. Even the event it shows is not secure in historical fact.

Many writers have tried to blacken Richard's name. At times, Richard must have had many enemies, perhaps because he offended people through being too tough. The Croyland chronicler presents an anti-Richard view before Tudor writers, like Thomas More, got to work. More wrote much stressing Richard's cruelty and the idea that he was a usurper, partly to make the Tudor dynasty seem more lawful.

On the other hand, there is much that is positive about Richard III. **Source B** says that he worked hard for the good of the north. Richard was a fine soldier and, after the Battle of Barnet (1471), in which he had fought bravely to help his brother, Richard was well rewarded. He received much land, like some of the Neville estates, as well as administrative positions of authority. Richard worked hard at his duties to make England safe. In 1480, he fought against the Scots, winning back Berwick in 1482. These are not like the actions of a cruel tyrant.

Source B expresses doubt about many of Richard's supposed crimes, including the murder of the Princes. This opinion should be the reliable work of a modern scholar basing his view on careful research.

Much of Richard's supposed cruelty may be explained by the fact that he was king in troubled times at the end of the Wars of the Roses. There remained much rivalry among the aristocracy and Richard's power was threatened by many 'over-mighty subjects'. To maintain his authority, Richard needed to be harsh and, at times, even cruel.

Richard's reputation was further blackened by fiction writers such as Shakespeare, who freely altered historical events to make his plays more dramatic. The idea of King Richard that most people still have is that of a deformed monster, based upon Shakespeare's play, *Richard III*.

The charge of 'ruthless usurper' murdering his way to the throne cannot be justified. The charge of being 'cruel', probably yes, at times, in order to maintain his position in a cruel and unsettled age.

Notes: _____

_____

_____

_____

_____

_____

_____

_____

_____

_____

_____

_____

ANSWERS TO EVIDENCE QUESTIONS
THE MAKING OF THE UNITED KINGDOM: 1485–1750

10 Henry VII, 1485–1509

→ Question

Using **ALL** the sources and your own knowledge, should Henry VII be remembered merely as a greedy king?

Answer

There is no doubt that Henry VII took a great interest in money. He loved money and he built up the wealth of the Crown. However, although finance was important to him, Henry VII had many other concerns.

Henry's keen interest in wealth is shown in **Source C**. The king carefully checked his accounts, noting all the payments to various people. His initials suggest that he was satisfied. **Source C** is a useful, official document which should be both reliable and accurate, at least if Henry VII thought so! The source confirms Henry's interest in money, but it does not necessarily signify greed.

The author of **Source A** also speaks of Henry's concern with money, but mainly 'in his later days'. This fully agrees with the view of **Source B** that the king gave way to avarice, but again, only in the final years of his reign.

Henry was concerned with much else besides money. The whole theme of his reign was that of building power, defeating his enemies and establishing and strengthening the position of the Tudor dynasty. **Source A** talks of his bravery and **B** says that by 1509 the main rebels were ruined. Crushing all forms of opposition was a major achievement of Henry, as Lambert Simnel and Perkin Warbeck found to their cost in 1487 and 1499 respectively.

Henry VII also developed trade, not only with the Netherlands, as in **Source B**, but also in the Baltic and the Mediterranean. The king also worked hard to strengthen law and order. According to **Source A**, 'he valued justice'. He used the law to strengthen his position through measures such as the Statutes of Livery and Maintenance and the *De Facto* Act (1495).

Protecting and maintaining religion was a key part of kingly duty at this period and **Source A** describes Henry as a 'passionate supporter of the Church'.

Both **Sources A** and **B** refer to Henry's interest in foreign policy. Henry used diplomacy and marriage agreements to strengthen England's reputation in Europe. He married Arthur, his eldest son, to Catherine of Aragon. After Arthur's death, Prince Henry was betrothed to the same princess. This brought links with Spain. The marriage of his daughter, Margaret, to James IV of Scotland helped to secure England's northern border, in theory at least. After a short war with France in 1492, Henry secured the Treaty of Etaples, which brought peace and reduced threats from Charles VIII. This treaty also closed France to Henry's Yorkist enemies. These were all notable achievements, outside finance.

Sources A and **B** should be accurate and reliable. Polydore Vergil had met Henry VII and knew about his character and widespread achievements. **Source B**, as the work of a modern historian, should be based on careful study to present an accurate version of events.

By 1509, Henry had indeed increased his revenue. The monarchy was in credit thanks to his care and concern with money. Perhaps, in his later years,

Henry VII was greedy, but there is little doubt that his achievements were many. Evidence, both from the sources and the wider story of history, strongly suggests that Henry VII should be remembered for far more than being 'merely' a greedy king.

Notes: _____

_____

_____

_____

_____

_____

_____

_____

_____

_____

_____

_____

_____

Henry VIII and Anne Boleyn

→ **Question**

Using **ALL** the sources and your own knowledge, is it true to say that Henry VIII divorced Catherine of Aragon only because he wanted an heir to the throne?

Answer

In May 1533, Henry VIII was finally able to divorce Catherine of Aragon and openly acknowledge Anne Boleyn as his queen. But was Henry driven to this divorce by new love or an intense desire to get a male heir? A strong case may be made for the latter view.

Source A offers plenty of material to support the idea that Henry VIII was driven by the wish to have a son. By 1527, Catherine was past having children. Henry needed a male heir. He saw the lack of a son as God's punishment for marrying Catherine in the first place, as his dead brother's widow, according to a verse which had been found in Leviticus. As the work of a modern historian writing a textbook, the information here should be accurate and reliable. This is a useful source for learning about what Henry wanted. What he wanted, above all else, was a son!

That the divorce proceeded despite desperate pleas by Catherine, and the delays of the Church court under Cardinal Campeggio, is shown in **Source C**, with Cranmer telling Catherine she was no longer Henry's wife. Catherine was angry at being put aside after Wolsey's failure to have the marriage annulled.

As a nineteenth-century picture, **Source C** is unreliable in this case. Its detail cannot be accurate. Nonetheless, it serves to give an impression of a sad event for Catherine.

However, perhaps it was fond love for Anne Boleyn which drove Henry forward to divorce Catherine. **Source A** describes how deeply in love with Anne Henry was. Royal love for Anne is again reflected in **Source B**. In this letter, Henry pours out his personal feelings in flowery phrases such as being 'pierced with the arrow of love' for over a year.

The truth of this source may be questioned. It is obviously biased as Henry is trying to persuade Anne to be his true love In such letters, anything can be written and there is no way of knowing whether Henry's feelings were true. This source says also that Henry gave Anne expensive presents such as golden brooches. Although the material strongly suggests that Henry wanted Anne, it does not reveal his motive.

Henry was always falling in and out of love with various ladies about the Court, as he even hints in **Source B**, saying that he would 'put all others who are about you' out of his thoughts if Anne would be his true love.

Although Henry was clearly attracted to Anne, the fact that, according to **Source A**, she was 'young enough to have children' was an added bonus. This perhaps spurred him on. From Anne, Henry thought he could have a son and heir. This intense wish led to his divorce from Catherine. What a shock then for Henry on that September afternoon in 1533 at Greenwich when Anne gave birth to a girl, the future Elizabeth I.

Three days after being born, Elizabeth was christened. Cranmer was among the godparents, but the king did not attend the ceremony. This suggests he was utterly disappointed. It was the desire for a male heir which had driven Henry to divorce Catherine of Aragon and not true love for Anne Boleyn. By the autumn of 1533, Henry's dynastic wish was again in tatters.

Notes: _____

_____

_____

_____

_____

_____

_____

_____

_____

_____

_____

_____

12 Henry VIII and the English Reformation, 1529–40

→ Question

Using **ALL** the sources and your own knowledge, how far is it true to say that Henry's desire for wealth was the main cause of the English Reformation?

Answer

Henry VIII's wish for wealth played a key part in bringing about the English Reformation up to 1540, but it may be argued that it was only one of many factors and not the main cause.

By the 1530s, Henry needed money. The Church was rich with access to a considerable income. **Source A** refers to the riches at Glastonbury. A large quantity of plate and £300 was found there, together with a golden chalice and several other valuable pieces which the abbot was supposed to have hidden.

This reference to monastic wealth agrees with **Source C** which shows a medieval shrine being dismantled by Thomas Cromwell's agents. Monasteries with such shrines had grown rich over time as pilgrims had made their gifts.

However, **Sources A** and **C** are unreliable and must be approached with care. **Source C** is an imaginary picture from the twentieth century. It is certainly not accurate in what it shows, although it does illustrate a true idea, namely that rich shrines were destroyed for the king to take the wealth.

Source A also needs to be used critically. Richard Layton, Cromwell's man, was determined to have Glastonbury closed down, so much of what he reported may have been false. He wanted to show the abbey as a rich and unholy place.

There is no doubt though that the Church at that time was wealthy. **Source B**, which is useful and reliable evidence based on research by a modern writer, notes that the Church owned about one-third of the country's land. Indeed, Cromwell's *Valor Ecclesiaticus* (1535) revealed the great wealth available in many churches and monasteries. This would have been attractive to Henry VIII who was much in need of extra funds.

However, it may be said that the king's wish for wealth was not the main cause of the English Reformation. Perhaps Henry's need for a male heir was the root cause? Catherine of Aragon seemed incapable of providing further children, so Henry required a new wife. To achieve this, he ultimately needed a new Church, because all attempts to settle his marital problems within the framework of Roman Catholicism had failed.

Once Henry thought about creating the Church *of* England and leaving the Church *in* England, several factors came into play to shape the English Reformation.

Protestant ideas, often based on the work of Martin Luther, circulated around Europe, in France and the German Empire. These crept into England to influence Henry and his advisers. English laymen resented paying tithes and Papal taxes and disliked the influence of a foreign Pope. They also hated Church courts where guilty clergy literally seemed to get away with murder. Many saw the clergy as no more than worthless layabouts (though some must have worked hard) and anticlericalism was common in many parts of the country. The Renaissance, too, played its part in making it easier to criticise the Catholic Church. Thus when Henry decided to set up his new Church, he found much to help him along the way.

The king's wish for wealth became a major incentive for religious change, but it was only one of many causes of the English Reformation and perhaps not even the main factor.

Notes: _____

_____

_____

_____

_____

_____

_____

_____

_____

_____

_____

13 Mary I and Lady Jane Grey

→ ## Question

Using **ALL** the sources and your own knowledge, how far do you agree that Mary I was right to execute Lady Jane Grey?

Answer

It may be argued that, by February 1554 Mary I was entirely right to execute Lady Jane Grey.

At the Tower of London, on 10 July 1553, Jane Grey had been proclaimed queen as part of a plot by the Duke of Northumberland to oust the Catholic Mary and replace her with a young Protestant ruler. Northumberland then hoped to control Jane through her marriage to his son, Lord Guilford Dudley.

Source B, a reliable and official document, is useful for showing us just how Jane saw herself politically. She took her claim to the throne seriously, referring to her 'rightful possession of the Kingdom' and to her 'just title'. Mary's rights are dismissed as 'false' and 'untrue'. Such comments reinforce the extent of Jane's political threat to Mary, encouraging Mary to take a harsh line.

However, by 19 July, Northumberland's schemes had failed. Jane was a prisoner and Mary was queen. It says much for Mary's mercy that, having been found guilty of treason and condemned, according to **Source A**, as early as November 1553, Jane was not executed earlier. Perhaps Mary was delaying matters? She was certainly showing mercy to Jane, a quality further illustrated by her treatment of the Kentish prisoners, as described in **Source A**. This evidence, from a modern historian, is useful for revealing the tolerant side of Mary. It is a reliable source, based upon research and careful study.

But then came Wyatt's Rebellion in January 1554. In this affair led by Thomas Wyatt, largely against Mary's proposed marriage to Philip II of Spain, the aim was to marry off Elizabeth to Edward Courtenay, a great-grandson of Edward IV, then put her on the throne instead of Mary. The fact that Jane was not involved in this plot, as mentioned in **Source A**, did not matter. Her father had tried unsuccessfully to raise rebels in Leicester. This was the final straw for Mary. Jane had to die, as she now 'represented too great a threat to live' as **Source A** further states.

Source C shows the outcome of Mary's fears. Its detail, as a nineteenth-century imaginative depiction of Jane on the way to her death, cannot be accurate. Nonetheless, this source illustrates a true event and a deed of cruel necessity.

Mary I had to execute Jane to maintain her political position as queen. She was also pressed to do so by many members of her Council who had opposed Northumberland's schemes. From her standpoint, Mary was also right to execute Jane for religious reasons. Jane Grey was Protestant. Mary was Catholic and, for her, the re-establishment of Roman Catholicism in England was everything she stood for.

The killing of a seventeen-year-old girl may seem cruel to modern eyes, but the harsh needs of Tudor politics and religion made it necessary. Mary had to survive. She had no choice but to do what she did, and she was absolutely right.

Mary I

Here are three attempts to answer this question, which reflect the different standards of answer as described in the ISEB mark scheme (see page 86). Pay particular attention to those at **Level 3**. This is the standard you are aiming for: the others are there to show you what **not** to do!

→ Question

Using **ALL** the sources and your own knowledge, was Mary I a cruel queen who failed in everything she tried to do?

Level 3 Answer

It may be argued that Mary Tudor was not a cruel queen, but that she did fail in all the important things she tried to do.

Source B shows Mary's harsh treatment of those people who failed to turn away from Protestantism. From this it would be easy to assume that she was cruel. Cranmer met a horrible death bravely. However, John Foxe produced his book in the reign of Elizabeth I. It was meant to glorify the sufferings of the Protestant Martyrs. In order to do this, their agonies were made to seem as brutal as possible. A major aim of this book was to highlight the violence of Mary's religious policy, and to make her appear as cruel as possible. On account of this, this source must be used with care.

C is another source suggesting that Mary was a cruel queen. Again, caution is required when forming an impression from it. As a picture produced long after the event it describes, it cannot be totally reliable. It will not be accurate in all its details.

However, we know that Mary burnt about 300 Protestant Martyrs in the fires of Smithfield. But was she really being cruel? That number of deaths over a period of three years is not many when compared with persecutions abroad. After all, death at the stake was the penalty laid down in the heresy laws of 1555. Mary was burning people to save the nation from mortal sin. It is also likely that she thought most people would change their religion rather than face the flames. By the standards of the age, Mary would not have appeared cruel. As it says in **Source A**, Mary kept to what she believed was the true faith and can be praised for this. Her motive was not cruelty.

On the other hand, Mary can be seen as a total failure in all her major policies. Even in religion her approach, as illustrated in **B** and **C**, helped to make Catholicism more unpopular and destroyed the very faith she was trying to preserve.

Mary failed to produce a Catholic heir. She also failed in her foreign policy. While supporting Spain, she involved England in a needless war against France. This resulted in the loss of Calais which the English had held since 1347. It was a humiliating disaster to lose it and broke the queen's heart.

In 1554, Mary had married Philip II of Spain. This 'Spanish Marriage' came to be hated and Philip was not allowed to remain in England. Through this marriage and the return to Catholicism, Mary generated a general fear of foreign domination by Spain and by the Pope. This increased her unpopularity. Mary also failed because she had lost the support of the very people who had welcomed her in 1553.

The small successes, with trade and some government reforms, as mentioned in **Source A**, were far outweighed by the large-scale failures in the same piece of evidence. This source should be reliable. The writer would have carried out precise research into many sources to ensure that the account is as accurate as possible. **Source A** does suggest that Mary was an overall failure.

In conclusion, although possibly not cruel, Mary was a failure in the main aspects of her reign. She failed the country and she failed to find personal happiness. Out of sympathy with England both by faith and by attitude, it was impossible for her to succeed.

Comments related to mark scheme

- Clear thesis at the start. (Mary not be a cruel queen, but a failure.)

- Well-structured answer.

- Clear conclusion referring back to the thesis stated at the start, which attempts a final judgement on the question statement.

- Valid arguments for and against the thesis.

- Valid and accurate use of own background knowledge to sustain and justify the thesis.

- Accurate and direct use of the sources to underpin the central thesis.

- Some cross-referencing of sources.

- Valid statements of reliability and utility of all the sources in relation to this specific question.

Level 2 answer

All the sources say that Mary Tudor was a cruel queen. This is stated at the beginning of **Source A**. **Source B** describes the horrible burning of Archbishop Thomas Cranmer because he would not change his religion back to being a Roman Catholic. This was a cruel thing for Mary to do and she did it in a cruel way by having Cranmer chained while he died. He was even pressed by Friar John until the very end to change his views. This could have made Cranmer's suffering worse.

The burning of several people at once, as shown in **Source C**, is another sign that Mary was a cruel queen. This source needs to be used with care. It is only a picture and was made a long time after Mary's reign.

Mary is supposed to have burnt more than 300 Protestants during her reign. Many of them were ordinary, poor people. There are some pictures of them being led to their executions, tied together with ropes.

The evidence also says that Mary failed in many of the important things she tried to do. In war against France, she lost Calais, as we see in **Source A**. Also, her marriage to Philip II of Spain was not liked in England.

Mary also failed to produce a Catholic heir to carry on her religion. So this was another important thing that Mary failed with. She also left England in debt because of her wars. She must have been unable to manage the county's money properly.

People hated her cruelty and they were very happy when she died in 1558 and Elizabeth I became queen. Elizabeth was a Protestant and by 1559 she had made England Protestant again. This undid all the work of Mary who tried to make England a Roman Catholic country. It proves that, in the end, Mary was a failure.

The sources show that Mary was cruel. They all show that the question is right and it is correct to say that Mary I was a cruel queen who failed in everything she tried to do.

Comments related to mark scheme

- No clear thesis at the start, although it is assumed from the writing that this answer will argue that Mary Tudor was a cruel queen.

- The sources are dealt with individually with little specific cross-referencing, despite a statement that they all show that Mary was cruel.

- The answer has some structure, based around the discussion of each source. This is then interspersed with own knowledge. None of this is developed fully enough in terms of answering the question exactly.

- Some relevant references to the source material to support the idea that Mary failed in some major aspects of her policy.

- There is one statement on the reliability of Source C but this is undeveloped. There are no further references concerning the provenance of any of the sources.

- A clear conclusion is offered in support of part of the question statement. This is good, but it is based on undeveloped argument and analysis.

Level 1 answer

Mary Tudor ruled from 1553 to 1558. She married Philip II of Spain who was a Roman Catholic. Mary wanted to make the whole of her kingdom Roman Catholic. Cardinal Pole helped her to do this. Mary thought that she was saving her country from mortal sin. A love of the Roman Catholic religion was the main thing which kept Mary going.

Mary burnt a lot of people (about 300) at Smithfield, in London. People were tied up to stakes. Sometimes people were burnt in groups as we can see in the picture. They were also burnt on their own like Thomas Cranmer.

Cranmer was burnt alive in Oxford in the town ditch. The place where he died is now called Broad Street and there is a cross in the road to mark the spot where he was executed.

Latimer and Ridley, who were bishops, were also burnt in Oxford in the year before Cranmer. All these men had refused to become Catholic from being Protestant, so Mary did not like them. Because the wood was damp and would not burn well, Ridley had a slow death. So they put a small barrel of gunpowder around his neck. When this exploded, it put an end to his suffering.

Mary was hated because of what she did to Protestants. She became unpopular. When she first became queen, she was liked by most of the people. Mary was made queen in place of Lady Jane Grey who was not the right queen even though she was a Protestant.

Mary also went to war with France and lost Calais, as it says in **Source A.** Mary said, 'When I die, Calais will be written on my heart.' This means that she knew she had upset the English people. England had owned Calais for a long time. It was a symbol of English power in France.

Mary was a cruel queen and she failed in everything that she did. So the question is right. Cardinal Pole died a few hours after Mary and all her wishes to make England a Catholic country again were not achieved. She was a failure as a queen. Mary was one of the worst queens England ever had.

Comments related to mark scheme

● A generalised answer.

● Some correct, general background knowledge, but it is not developed or applied directly to the specific needs of the question.

● Too much time wasted by including irrelevant material, such as the reference to Lady Jane Grey.

● No links are made between the sources and own knowledge.

● There are hardly any references to the sources.

● No cross-referencing of the sources.

● No evaluation of the utility of the sources.

● Little apparent structure to the main body of the answer.

● No initial, central idea or thesis to sustain the argument.

● There is a firm conclusion and it is related to the question, but it appears out of nowhere. It does not follow logically from the paragraphs which come before it.

Notes: _____

_____

_____

_____

_____

_____

_____

_____

_____

_____

_____

15 Elizabeth I and Mary Stuart

→ **Question**

Using **ALL** the sources and your own knowledge, do you think that Elizabeth I was right to execute Mary?

Answer

The general historical background and the sources suggest that Elizabeth I was indeed right to execute Mary Stuart.

It may also be argued that Elizabeth was reluctant to kill her cousin; that she thought carefully about it and that the final decision was based on pressure from her councillors.

Source C certainly supports this view. The queen looks thoughtful and in no mood to rush to sign the papers. Lord Burghley seems to be pressing her. As a twentieth-century picture, **Source C** cannot be an accurate representation of what actually took place. We do not know for certain what Burghley said. Nonetheless, the source gives a vivid impression of what may have happened and, as such, it is useful if considered carefully.

This idea of pressure from councillors is echoed in **Source B**. Walsingham refers to Mary Stuart as 'that devilish woman'. He clearly wanted her dead so that Elizabeth's subjects could live in peace and safety.

But despite her reluctance or any pressure she may have faced, Elizabeth was right to execute Mary Stuart. **Source B** refers to Mary as having agents in touch with both France and Scotland and that she was receiving cash from Paris to help her schemes. Perhaps she was plotting?

Mary was a huge political threat to Elizabeth. She had a strong claim to the throne, especially with the queen unmarried and with no heir. Some Catholics did not even see Elizabeth as the true queen. **Source B** further relates that Mary's very 'existence' endangered that of the queen, an indication that her execution was right. As the work of a modern historian the evidence in **Source B** ought to be reliable, as based on careful research in pursuit of the truth.

Source A speaks of 'various ways and manners' which hint at some of the schemes to place Mary on the throne. Mary was associated with many of these such as the Northern Rebellion (1569), the Ridolfi and Throckmorton Plots of 1571 and 1583 and the great Babington Conspiracy (1586), each of which planned to oust Elizabeth in favour of Mary Stuart.

It has been said that some evidence of Mary's involvement in these plots was forged by Burghley's agents in an effort to get her removed from the political scene. The truth of this is hard to determine. But Elizabeth evidently felt threatened. In **Source A**, she writes of Mary's 'attempts' to take her life. This material requires careful interpretation. It is biased because Elizabeth wrote it. However, it usefully indicates exactly what the queen thought.

Mary was also a political danger to Elizabeth because of her position in the dynastic struggles between England, Scotland and France.

As a Roman Catholic, Mary posed a religious threat. Elizabeth as Supreme Governor of the Church of England had a duty to protect the religion of the nation. This could be in danger while Mary lived. Mary also remained a focus for more possible Roman Catholic plots. Elizabeth, by 1586, had faced enough of these.

Overall, it may be argued that Mary Stuart's execution was a necessary political action. Elizabeth I really had no choice in the matter. For the maintenance of her position as queen, the signing of Mary Stuart's death warrant was absolutely right.

Notes: _____

_____

_____

_____

_____

_____

_____

_____

_____

_____

_____

_____

_____

16 The causes of the English Civil War, 1629–42

→ Question

....

Using **ALL** the sources and your own knowledge, do you agree that the English Civil War was caused largely by the actions of royal ministers and parliamentary leaders?

Answer

Although it is sensible to argue that the English Civil War was largely caused by the actions of royal ministers and parliamentary leaders, there were other factors which contributed to the conflict.

First, the character of the king; Charles I was stubborn and inflexible in his approach. Thus, for some, war became the only realistic way out of the current political dispute. Second, Charles's belief in the Divine Right theory helped generate further tension which led to war. The king saw himself as appointed by God and felt answerable to him alone, hence his utter contempt for much of the parliamentary opposition. It was partly as a reaction to this that parliament took such drastic action against Charles's government and ministers, as illustrated in **Sources B** and **C**.

External factors also played a part in causing war. The Scots rebelled in 1639 and 1640, leading to the need for a parliament which eventually fought and defeated the king. The Irish Rebellion (1641) produced arguments over the control of the army, another factor in the lead-up to war. However, it may be said that both the Scottish and the Irish rebellions were partly the result of the work of Laud and Strafford respectively.

Indeed, the policies and attitudes of the king's chief ministers were a major cause of the war. Laud upset English Puritans, Roman Catholics and Scots by his insistence on High Church Anglican policies to promote 'the beauty of holiness', as well as his belief in ruling the Church through bishops.

Source A shows Laud's ideas. It reveals his total belief in Anglican doctrine and in the use of bishops to govern the Church. The nature of this source is important. It is an oath and it gives the impression that it is to be forced on people whether they like it or not. It reveals Laud's strict, authoritarian approach to religion. **Source A** is reliable, if biased. It is useful to show us what Laud wanted.

Source C, although not accurate in its detail, is useful in depicting a true event. It shows what happened to Strafford, who had served Charles through his tough policy of 'Thorough'. That Strafford was executed reveals the unpopularity both of a royal minister and his policies. **Source C** shows the results of a tough policy, whereas **Source A** shows a tough policy being prepared.

However, parliamentary leaders, too, played their part in generating Civil War. Pym and Hampden forced the pace of opposition to the king after November 1640.

As mentioned in **Source B**, 'a series of Acts was ... passed in the summer of 1641'. By these, the mechanism of Personal Rule was dismantled. Ship Money was ended, as were the Courts of Star Chamber and High Commission and all methods of raising taxes without parliament's approval. As the source continues, 'many in parliament wished to limit the king's powers'. Such measures made war increasingly likely. There seemed no other way out for Charles.

Source B is both useful for its content and reliable as the work of a modern writer who will have studied carefully before setting out the material.

Not content with the summer measures of 1641, the parliamentary leaders produced the Grand Remonstrance (November 1641), followed by the Nineteen Propositions (June 1642), which tried to place even more restrictions on Charles's kingly power. Charles felt pushed to the limit, thus he declared war on Parliament in August 1642.

Overall, despite other factors, it does seem fair to argue that war came in 1642 largely owing to the antagonistic actions of both royal ministers and parliamentary leaders.

Notes: _____

_____

_____

_____

_____

_____

_____

_____

_____

_____

_____

17 The execution of Charles I

→ Question

Using **ALL** the sources and your own knowledge, how far do you agree that Charles I was a hated tyrant and traitor who deserved to die in 1649?

Answer

Charles I was not a hated tyrant who deserved to die in 1649. The fact that Charles was called 'a tyrant, traitor and murderer and a public and implacable enemy to the Commonwealth of England' should not be taken literally. These words are from the prosecutor's charge at his trial. The prosecution described Charles using words to make him seem as evil as possible.

Source A says that Charles thought he was dying for the 'liberty and freedom' of his people. These are not the ideas of a traitor or tyrant. The source describes how some people dipped their handkerchiefs in the royal blood as a mark of respect or as protection against illness. These are not the actions of people who hate their king.

As evidence from a modern textbook, **Source A** should be reliable. The author will have studied carefully to try to produce an accurate and truthful narrative.

Source B agrees with **Source A** in recounting people's affection for the king. There were 'open marks of sorrow' at his death. Some people became sad, ill or even died of grief! This evidence needs to be read with care. Much is exaggerated. Echard, writing long after Charles's execution, would seem to be a biased royalist. Nonetheless, the overall impression is of a people fond of their king, as shown through their sorrow at his death.

This idea of sadness at the king's execution is repeated in **Source C**. That the crowd let out a huge groan is a sign that they were upset. **Source C** shows a mass of people at Whitehall who came to pay their last respects to Charles I.

As an eighteenth-century illustration based on an earlier picture, **Source C** may not be totally accurate. It needs to be looked at carefully. However, it gives a general impression of the execution, with some people so upset that they fainted. Thus, all the sources agree in suggesting that Charles I was not hated and that many of his people were distressed by his death.

On the other hand, while perhaps not a tyrant, Charles had disregarded parliament during his period of Personal Rule (1629–40). During that time, he relied heavily on two chief ministers, Strafford and Laud, who respectively controlled the State and the Church. Operating through the Prerogative Courts of Star Chamber and High Commission, they bypassed the Common Law to raise taxes without Parliament's consent. Did this make the king a tyrant? Perhaps not; his power was soon reduced by the Long Parliament.

It may be argued, too, that Charles's declaration of war against parliament was not an act of tyranny. It was made, as **Source A** states, in the interests of the 'liberty and freedom' of his people.

There is no doubt that Charles through his ministers had, at times, appeared tough. However, he cannot really be described as a tyrant and he was certainly no traitor to his people. There are examples in all the sources of people's affection for him. Charles was not hated and many believed he did not deserve to die in 1649.

18 The Plague of London, 1665

→ Question

···

Using **ALL** the sources and your own knowledge, how true is it to say that the spread of the Great Plague in London was caused by a lack of proper medical knowledge?

Answer

There is no doubt that the extension of the plague was caused by a lack of proper medical knowledge, but this was only one of many factors in the spread of the disease.

Source A says that medical knowledge was 'primitive' and that there was little awareness of hygiene. It mentions that even intelligent, educated men such as Pepys wore special good-luck charms to keep away the disease. Some thought that the visitation of the plague was God's punishment for the sins of the world. There was also a view that it was all fixed in the stars. All this shows little understanding of the real causes of the disease.

As the work of a modern historian, **Source A** provides much useful information. It should also be reliable material, based on the results of thorough research and study.

This agrees well with **Source B**. Hodges describes how fires were lit in the streets to purify the air and how the precautions taken by the London authorities failed to halt the spread of the disease. Again, in **Source B**, we have the idea that God was angry, as implied in **Source A**, and that he could be soothed by 'Publick Prayers'.

Source B is an honest and reliable account written in good faith, about what was done to combat the plague. As such it is useful in telling us something about the extent of seventeenth-century medical knowledge.

In his account, Hodges offers cures for the plague. Some are sensible, such as separating the sick from the well, maintaining personal cleanliness and ridding the streets of filth, 'Stench and Nastiness'. However, most of his remedies, which included possets, milk drinks, sweating and bleeding the patient to drive out the 'Morbid Humours' would have been ineffective.

Other factors influencing the spread of the disease are illustrated in **Source C**. As a nineteenth-century engraving, the scene it shows is imaginary. Nonetheless, it depicts some important reasons for the spread of the plague which may be supported from other sources such as Pepys's *Diary*.

In **Source C**, we see how close together the houses were. We note, too, the general level of dirt with a sewage channel running down the road and dead bodies lying about the street. This would have helped disease to spread.

Pepys wrote of people full of sores lying in the road and of crowds attending funerals, with bodies being freely carried through the streets. Pepys also describes fires to purify the air, as mentioned in **Source B**. Yet another ineffective plague remedy.

Hodges in his account of the plague mentions the killing of cats and dogs. This agrees with **Source A** in that some animals were thought to carry the disease. But as acknowledged in **Source A**, there is no mention of the rats.

In conclusion, the evidence from a wide range of sources suggests that the spread of the Great Plague of London was due to many other factors than merely a lack of proper medical knowledge.

Notes: _____

_____

_____

_____

_____

_____

_____

_____

_____

_____

_____

_____

19 The Fire of London, 1666

→ Question

Using **ALL** the sources and your own knowledge, how far was the Great Fire of 1666 a total disaster for London?

Answer

In the short term, the Great Fire was a total disaster for London. However, over time, the city rose from the ashes and recovered. The fire even opened up new chances for improvement.

The initial disaster is well illustrated in **Sources B** and **C**. The evidence in **Source B** is based on John Evelyn's eyewitness account as he walked through the ruins on Friday 7 September, just six days after the fire broke out. This is a useful and accurate source, which gives a picture of the devastation together with some personal comments. There is no reason to doubt his observations.

From **Source B**, we learn of the extent of the physical destruction. Indeed, some 87 parish churches and more than 13,000 houses were consumed by the flames. So was old St Paul's. Miraculously, only about four or five people died. Nonetheless, the fire was a huge disaster, destroying more than 80 per cent of the City within the walls, according to **Source C**.

Such devastation led to much social hardship as people were made homeless. Evelyn's *Diary* says that large stately houses as well as 'the sheds of the poor' were destroyed together and that the City was burnt 'without distinction'.

Source C shows the destruction. As a picture painted soon after the event, it is a useful piece of evidence. The horror and extent of the fire are shown, as well as people in the river and on the banks trying to save their possessions. Such scenes are described also in the *Diary* of Samuel Pepys. But **Source C** cannot be accurate in every detail and must be used with care.

The Great Fire was also an economic disaster. Trade was interrupted. **Source B** tells of the destruction of many of the Livery Companies' Halls and warehouses. The Guildhall and the Royal Exchange were ruined, as well as the premises of small craftsmen. Such people then lost their means of making a living.

But from this disaster came new opportunities, as outlined in **Source A**. This material, supplied by a modern writer, should be accurate and reliable as the result of the author's studies. **Source A** offers a positive slant on the fire.

Christopher Wren in 1673 began to rebuild St Paul's. This was completed by 1711. Its dome remains today as one of the key landmarks in London. **Source A** also mentions Wren's construction of new parish churches. Some of these, like St Mary-Le-Bow and St Bride's, are noted for their wonderful steeples.

Ordinary houses were improved with a more widespread use of brick to reduce the fire risks. Even though Wren's great scheme to rebuild the City was never completed, many streets were widened and much of the filth of earlier years was cleared away. For a time, London became a healthier place to live in.

Trade gradually resumed. The Guildhall was quickly rebuilt along with many of the Livery Companies' Halls. After the disruption of 1666, London recovered.

In conclusion, it may be argued that, although seeming a complete disaster at the time, the Great Fire opened up new opportunities for London so that by the eighteenth century, it was again a prosperous and flourishing city.

Notes: _____

_____

_____

_____

_____

_____

_____

_____

_____

_____

_____

_____

_____

John Churchill, Duke of Marlborough

→ Question

Using **ALL** the sources and your own knowledge, how important was the Battle of Blenheim in the War of the Spanish Succession?

Answer

The Battle of Blenheim was of the highest importance to England and to Europe as a whole both in the short and long term.

In the short term, Blenheim was an overwhelming victory for the Allies and Marlborough. The extent of the French defeat is shown in **Source C**. Tallard, the French commander, was captured, together with numerous regimental colours and a mass of French treasure.

Source C, even as a painting produced soon after the battle, may not be accurate in all its details. Nevertheless in illustrating Marlborough's victory, it shows some well-known military events.

Writing to his wife after the battle, Marlborough himself claimed that 'never was victory so complete'. Furthermore, Queen Anne was to be informed that her army had had 'a glorious victory'.

This short-term military success is reflected in **Source A** which describes the battle as 'decisive' and Louis XIV as 'humbled'. The myth of French invincibility had been shattered and England had gained military greatness.

Blenheim was a victory, too, in diplomatic terms. England's allies, the Dutch and some German Princes, were strengthened. So also was the whole idea of using an alliance to counter Louis XIV's threats.

Source A further speaks of the Empire being saved and of democracy being strengthened. As evidence from a modern historical scholar, **Source A** should be accurate and reliable. It is certainly useful for gauging the importance of the battle.

There were other short-term gains. In religion, the English Protestant Succession was strengthened. In political terms, England's reputation and prestige in Europe increased as did that of her government and monarch.

Blenheim was important, too, in the longer term. The Allies received a huge injection of military confidence. From 1704, their armies now believed they could beat the French. This served to make them conquerors in the war. This new spirit is described in **Source B**. As the reflections of a man present at Blenheim who well knew the feelings of the army, this evidence ought to be reliable. True, it was published sometime after the events it describes, but even as one of Marlborough's soldiers, the author had little cause to lie.

This new sense of military confidence certainly paid dividends. Blenheim was a turning point in the War of the Spanish Succession, putting the Allies on the road to further victories such as those at Ramillies (1706), Oudenarde (1708) and Malplaquet (1709). By then France was ready for peace. This came with the Treaty of Utrecht in 1713.

The settlement was a triumph for England with territorial gains like Gibraltar and Nova Scotia, which laid the foundations for what eventually became the British Colonial Empire.

The importance of the Battle of Blenheim is not confined to England. The United Provinces and the German Empire had been saved from French threats.

The ambitions of a country trying to upset the European balance of power had been thwarted. In this sense, the Battle of Blenheim was of vital importance to England and the rest of Europe, both in 1704 and in the decades which followed.

Notes: _____

_____

_____

_____

_____

_____

_____

_____

_____

_____

_____

_____

_____

The Jacobite Rebellion, 1745

21

➔ Question

Using **ALL** the sources and your own knowledge, how far do you consider the Jacobite Rebellion of 1745 a real threat to George II and his government?

Answer

It may be argued that for a short time in the early stages of the Jacobite Rebellion some contemporaries saw it as a real threat to George II and his government. However, long before Culloden, any realistic challenge to royal authority was over. If anything, George II was strengthened by a rebellion which failed.

Horace Walpole, writing in December 1745, initially saw the Jacobites as a threat. After victory at Prestonpans in September, the Jacobites had marched south causing panic as a succession of towns fell. Walpole was worried. His letter, **Source B**, is accurate and reliable in general terms. He had no reason to be untruthful to his friend. **Source B** is certainly useful in telling us how contemporaries felt. Clearly there was a sense of fear and panic as the rebels advanced.

Fear of the Jacobites was increased by their victory at Prestonpans, as shown in **Source C**. Here, the Jacobites deployed their standard military tactic of the Highland Charge which routed Sir John Cope's troops. **Source C**, as a nineteenth-century image of the battle, is hardly accurate in its details. It gives a romanticised view and should be used with care. Nonetheless, it illustrates a true event: a victory for Bonnie Prince Charlie, further fuelling English fears as the Jacobites decided to march south.

But the march south failed. There was no depth of popular support for their cause in England. Even the Jacobites were split over the decision to march on London. Thus in December 1745, on the advice of Lord George Murray, the Jacobites turned back at Derby. 'We dread them no longer' wrote a relieved Horace Walpole. The retreat from Derby marked the high-water mark of any Jacobite threat.

Despite commenting that the rising 'came astonishingly close to success', **Source A** argues that without large-scale French help, the prospects of a Jacobite victory were destroyed. Furthermore, as **Source A** continues, the English Catholics were reluctant to join the rising.

As the work of a modern historian, based on careful study and research, **Source A** is valuable. It should be accurate and reliable. Overall, it makes the clear point that the rebels were unable to 'force their case'.

Thus the Jacobites were never a genuine long-term threat to George II, despite their initial successes as they raised their standard at Glenfinnan, captured Edinburgh, won victory at Prestonpans and even snatched a win at Falkirk in January 1746 during their final retreat north. The rebels were constantly short of supplies and support. Their threat became less as the rebellion proceeded. They were eventually annihilated at Culloden by Cumberland and his army in April 1746.

Even the very cause of Jacobitism was past its day. England wanted peace. Protestantism and the Hanoverians were strong, perhaps stronger still after 1746 and the subsequent Highland Clearances.

The 1745 Rebellion has been called the 'Rash Adventure'. It was indeed rash. George II and his government were never seriously threatened.

Notes: _____

_____

_____

_____

_____

_____

_____

_____

_____

_____

_____

_____

_____

ANSWERS TO EVIDENCE
QUESTIONS
BRITAIN AND EMPIRE:
1750–1914

22 The causes of the American War of Independence, 1763–76

→ Question

Using **ALL** the sources and your own knowledge, how far is it true to say that American opposition to British taxation was the main cause of the American War of Independence?

Answer

It is debatable whether American opposition to British taxation was 'the' main cause of the American War of Independence. Such an important event had many causes. However, opposition to British taxes was certainly 'an' important cause. It increased Anglo-Colonial tensions throughout the 1760s and 1770s. It served also to give a sense of focus to American hostility to British policies.

Source C provides a vivid illustration of the idea of American opposition and of the tensions which British taxes were generating. As a modern picture, the source is hardly accurate in all its details. Nonetheless, it is useful in showing a true historical event. It also puts the abstract idea of American opposition into concrete terms.

The Boston Tea Party was part of a series of aggressive reactions to British taxation. Such was the opposition to the Stamp Act (1765), for example, that it was repealed the following year only to be replaced with a Declaratory Act, which enraged the colonists. Then came the hated Townshend Duties of 1767, which further increased tension.

British retaliation to the Boston protest took the form of the Coercive Acts against the supposedly dangerous state of Massachusetts. While mainly suppressing political rights, this legislation was also linked to Boston's resistance to British taxation.

However, opposition to British taxes had a wider importance than finance. It gave a sense of unity and focus to other factors. Political thinkers such as Samuel Adams and Thomas Paine were considering throwing off British rule to allow the Colonies to manage themselves. **Source A** mentions a 'mature and powerful English-speaking community with a mind of its own' looking to manage its future. The source also speaks of the increasing 'unity of action' among many colonists as the result of the 'repressive actions of the British government'. The formation of such colonial attitudes was another outcome of British tax policies.

As the work of a modern historian, even though from an American viewpoint, this source should be accurate and truthful. The author will have researched carefully in order to produce a fair account.

That the Colonies were developing their own 'mind' is further reflected in **Source B**. This speech by Adams is obviously biased as he is pressing his case. Its language is aggressive with phrases like 'Britain has treated us as beasts of burden'. However, this is both reliable and useful. It shows us the intense passions aroused in colonial minds by Britain's uncompromising attitude and policies. For Adams and others, independence was the only way forward and for that, in view of George III's stubborn approach to the American situation, war became the only method.

Thus American opposition to British taxation was an important cause of the war. Of itself it increased tension between Britain and the American colonies. It also helped to shape individual colonial attitudes and ideas into a single statement of intent. This presented itself in July 1776 as the American Declaration of Independence. Britain then had no option but to fight a full-scale war.

Notes: _____

_____

_____

_____

_____

_____

_____

_____

_____

_____

_____

_____

23 The Transport Revolution

Here are three attempts to answer this question, which reflect the different standards of answer as described in the ISEB mark scheme (see page 86). Pay particular attention to those at **Level 3**. This is the standard you are aiming for: the others are there to show you what **not** to do!

→ Question

Using **ALL** the sources and your own knowledge, were the railways welcomed by all?

Level 3 answer

As part of the transport revolution there was a rapid expansion of railways during the nineteenth century especially after the 'Railway Mania' of the 1840s. Railways brought great benefits, but they were not welcomed by all.

Manufacturers and traders were keen on railways, as we see from **Sources A** and **B**. Goods could be carried quickly to the ports. This would mean better markets for traders as they could sell more and increase their business. Farmers, too, could benefit by using railways to send their produce to wider markets, as stated in **Source B**. Farmers might even gain by more easily bringing in supplies such as manure and lime for their farms, again as stated in **Source B**.

Source A is useful for seeing who favoured the railways. It was written by a modern historian who will have done research and tried to be accurate and find out the truth. **Source B**, on the other hand, must be used with care. It is not so reliable. It was produced by a railway company keen to show all the supposed benefits of a scheme not yet carried out. It is almost like an advertisement. As such, it could be biased.

The coming of the railways brought many other benefits. More iron and coal were needed, so these industries were boosted. Engines were using over one million tons of coal a year by 1850. More people could travel more easily. Seaside resorts, such as Scarborough and Blackpool, expanded (as mentioned in **Source A**) and soccer became England's national game as leagues were set up now that teams could travel easily to away matches. Food like fish could be sent to more parts of the country in a fresh condition. More jobs were created, both in building and running the system. New railway towns, such as Crewe and Swindon, grew up and flourished.

However, the railways were not welcomed by everyone. **Source A** mentions opposition from canal companies as their trade declined. Canal shares fell, such as those of the Grand Junction Canal Company, which went down from a top level of £330 to £70 by 1853.

Source A speaks of opposition from coach companies and toll collectors as well as some of the aristocracy, like the Duke of Wellington, who resisted railway growth as it might encourage the lower classes to travel about more.

As we have suggested, **Source A** should be reliable. Inn keepers along many old main roads which became deserted also suffered great losses of income and trade.

Opposition to new railways is also clearly shown in **Source C**. The *Punch* cartoon is not accurate in its actual details, but the idea behind it is probably true. Cartoons often reflect the reality of the time. The railways were hated by those who feared change or whose way of making a living was threatened. *Punch* suggests that the opposition forces would eventually be run over.

In conclusion, despite all the benefits from the coming of the railways and their development to modern times, it is not true to say that they were welcomed by all. Although opposition was overcome, it was considerable at times as the railway system developed.

Comments related to mark scheme

● Strong introduction to set the scene and a clear thesis.

● Well-structured discussion. Those welcoming the railways are considered first, followed by the opponents.

● Clear cross-referencing of sources.

● Valid statements on the reliability and utility of all the sources.

● Valid and relevant use of own background knowledge to underpin the discussion and analysis.

● Strong conclusion relating back to the introduction and offering a reasoned judgement in relation to the question statement.

Level 2 answer

Sources like **A** and **B** show that some people welcomed the coming of the railways. **Source A** also mentions that there was opposition and this is supported by **Source C**.

Source C illustrates a man on a horse dressed as a medieval knight with his armour. Perhaps he represents the old ways. The knight is trying to stop the advance of progress as shown by the railway engine. It seems as though he is about to be crushed by the train. This picture suggests that not everyone welcomed the railways.

The idea of resistance to the railways is also mentioned in **Source A**. The author says that landowners and canal companies resented the growth of the railway network. This was because trains were faster than canals. So, as more people started to use them, canal trade dropped. This is shown by the fall in the value of canal shares. For example, the share price of the Grand Junction Canal Company fell from a high of £330 to £70 by 1853.

People who owned coaching companies also hated the trains because they were quicker, so more passengers preferred to use them. **Source A** also says that many of the great old roads became deserted. The inn-keepers along those roads would not like this. Fewer travellers staying in their rooms would mean a fall in income.

But there were lots of people who did welcome railway development. Obviously, railway companies did, like the one in **Source B**, which outlines the benefits of the railway to farmers, landowners, traders and the general public.

Source A also says that trade expanded and that towns like Swindon developed. People living around London liked the new railways as they could get to work more easily as commuters.

Others, like Brunel, welcomed the railways because they made lots of money out of them. Brunel developed the Great Western Railway and he built magnificent stations at Paddington and Bristol.

Many ordinary people liked railways. After an Act of 1844, they could travel more cheaply to the new seaside towns like Scarborough and Brighton. Ordinary people could also get jobs on the railway. Lots of navvies were needed to build the tunnels, cuttings and embankments, as well as the bridges and viaducts. By 1851, over 60,000 people were involved with the railway network.

Some of the upper classes, though, did not welcome the coming of railways. In **Source A**, the Duke of Wellington disliked the idea of more travel for the 'lower classes'. Other noblemen tried to prevent railway lines from crossing their land.

There was much opposition, too, in beautiful parts of the country such as the Lake District. People there thought that the railway lines with their noise, smoke, viaducts and bridges would ruin the peace and beauty of the landscape.

Not everyone wanted the trains. So, from the question, it is not true to say that the railways were welcomed by all as part of a transport revolution.

Comments related to mark scheme

- The introduction clearly recognises that there are two sides to the question of railway development, but no definite thesis is offered.

- This leads to some of the material 'floating about' in the answer without a sense of purpose. An exact thesis would have given direction to much of what is written here.

- Some notable comprehension of the sources (as with Source C) with relevant comment linked to the question. Comments could be developed further.

- Some relevant links between own knowledge and the question.

- Some cross-referencing of the sources, particularly between A and C.

- Some flashes of reasoned analysis, but an overall lack of structure detracts from the general effect.

- The conclusion offers an opinion which is relevant to the question statement.

- Nothing concerning the provenance, reliability or utility of the sources which places this answer firmly at Level 2.

Level 1 answer

Source A says that rich dukes, coaching companies and owners of canals did not like the railways. The man on the horse in **Source C**, who is dressed as a medieval knight, is trying to stop the train with his lance, which looks like part of an old branch.

There are those in **Source B** who want the railways. This is because they are a railway company planning a new line from Liverpool to Manchester. They say that this line will be good for farmers who will be able to buy manure and sell more of their crops. It will also be better for the public to travel and coal will be cheaper.

People in **Source A** who welcome the railways include manufacturers and other men in business. There was urban growth and some old towns got better. Many new towns grew up, like Swindon which was connected with the railway and Blackpool, Scarborough and Bournemouth where people could go on holiday.

The Liverpool to Manchester Railway, mentioned in **Source B**, was opened eventually in 1830. This was followed in 1839 by the London to Birmingham line. By 1851, there were nearly 7,000 miles of track and big towns such as

York, Leeds, Carlisle, Newcastle, Hull and Birmingham all had railways and were linked.

There was some opposition, as shown in **Source C**, but the railways came and brought lots of good things for many people.

George Hudson was known as the 'Railway King' because he did many good things for the railways in the north of England until he ran out of money. Another important railway person was Isambard Kingdom Brunel who built a big tunnel near Bath.

More ordinary people could travel as railways developed and there was a new social mobility. New political ideas could spread quickly. The coal industry welcomed the railways because more coal was needed for the trains. Lots of iron was needed, too, to make the engines, bridges and stations. People who made bricks sold them to the railways for the new viaducts like the one at Stockport which has 27 arches.

Fresh food was more available and things that easily went bad, like fish, meat and fruit were transported more quickly around the country. Ordinary people now had better things to eat. Many people welcomed the railways because they could get jobs either building or running the system. Even Queen Victoria liked the trains and went on a trip to Windsor.

There was not much opposition and railways were welcomed by all as the question says.

Comments related to mark scheme

● No introduction or stated thesis.

● Some selection of material in relation to the question, as in the first paragraph about those who opposed the railways.

● Some recognition of the significance of a source, as in the second paragraph regarding the obvious support for railways by the railway company.

● Failure to use the content of the sources in a way relevant to the question.

● The sources are merely described. There is little sense of evaluation or interpretation.

● No direct cross-referencing of the sources.

● No reference to the provenance, reliability or utility of any of the sources.

● The answer is unbalanced. Opposition to the development of railways is brushed aside after the opening paragraph. There are also contradictions concerning opposition to railways.

● The answer drifts into a general account of the benefits brought by the railways. Some material is detailed; but knowledge is random and not related specifically to the question.

● There is a sense that the writer does not fully understand some of what has been revised. 'Social mobility' sits awkwardly in the sentence.

● Too many of the sentences are too vague.

● There is little structure. The sources are cast aside after some simple comment. The impression is that the writer has seen the word 'railways' (a revised topic) and then decided to write a piece on railways without any regard for the question.

● The final judgement is too general. It does not come logically from the main body of the answer.

● In the final judgement, there is an indication that the writer had not understood the exact point of the question.

→ Question

Using **ALL** the sources and your own knowledge, did the Reform Bill really bring much change?

Answer

It may be argued that although the Reform Bill did not bring as much change in 1832 as radical reformers wanted, the very passing of the Bill showed that political change was possible. The carrying through of the Bill also represented an important shift in upper-class outlook and led to long-term political benefits for all.

Source A provides much concerning the political and social change resulting from the Bill. It says that the Bill was never intended to give all men the vote. Women, of course, were never considered at this date!

The changes, both in boroughs and the countryside as outlined in **Source A**, meant that only the better sort of villager or townsman gained the vote. Overall, the middle classes benefited as did some industrialists. However, change was limited. The working class gained nothing and the great landowners still dominated Parliament.

As the work of a modern historian, this material is useful and reliable, based as it should be on careful reading and research. It is thus a valuable source in helping to understand the extent of political change in 1832. And there *was* change.

Through the Bill, boroughs with fewer than 2,000 people lost both their MPs. This enabled the redistribution of 143 parliamentary seats to growing centres such as Manchester and Sheffield. Thus industrial interests were better represented. Also, as a result of the Bill, about one-sixth of the male population had the right to vote.

Much, though, was not done. No secret ballot was introduced and generally, the Bill was not far-reaching enough for radicals such as William Cobbett and Henry Hunt. Such men were disappointed. With much revolutionary activity abroad, there was a widespread fear of disorder in Britain.

Source C illustrates this disorder in Bristol. The details of the picture are perhaps not accurate, but such scenes were enough to frighten the upper classes. The evidence is thus useful to show clearly a picture of social unrest.

Source B shows the fears (perhaps based on such scenes as **Source C**), which coloured the attitude of some genteel reformers. Was Macaulay a genuine reformer, or did he support reform out of fear? As he says, the Bill was 'security against a revolution' and a means of preserving the upper and middle classes. Macaulay seems to be expressing an honest opinion. **Source B** thus offers a reliable insight into the minds of the upper classes and explains in part why the Bill was passed. Upper-class self-interest and self-preservation seemed to play a vital part!

Although in 1832 change was limited, the key point is that some change had been made. The idea of political change and of widening the right to vote had become a reality. This idea became increasingly real with the reforms of

1867, 1884, suffrage for men and women over 21 in 1928, and voting for all aged over 18 in 1969.

It may be said that the 1832 Reform Bill was a catalyst. Though its immediate effects may have seemed modest, in the longer term the change it helped to bring about was considerable.

Notes: _____

_____

_____

_____

_____

_____

_____

_____

_____

_____

_____

_____

The Chartists

→ Question

Using **ALL** the sources and your own knowledge, how far do you consider Chartism a failure?

Answer

After the rejection by parliament of the third Petition in 1848, Chartism looked a failure. However, when examined in the longer term, the success of many of its initial ideas becomes apparent.

Chartism began when William Lovett led a working-class group to seek the vote for all men. In 1836, the London Working Men's Association set out its six demands. They wanted: universal male suffrage, equal electoral districts, annual parliaments, the payment of MPs, a secret ballot and the end of the property qualification for MPs. Their ideal was to attain political power as the first stage of making a new economic order in society. By 1838, the movement had spread to Birmingham.

This growth may be noted in **Sources B** and **C**. In **Source B**, Thomas Attwood claims that more than one million people had signed the first Petition of 1839. The figure in the source is probably not accurate, but it serves its purpose by allowing comparison with the over 3 million mentioned in **Source C**. The details of **Source C** are perhaps not exact either, but there does seem to be a large pile of paper in the middle of the House of Commons! **Source C** must be used with care, but it is useful to illustrate the idea that Chartism was backed.

Source B is of course biased. Attwood as a Chartist supporter is doing his best to present their case to Parliament. It is notable that he stresses that Chartists were 'honest and industrious' and sober men who always obeyed the laws.

This was probably to reduce government suspicion of the movement generated by riots like those in Newport (1839) and by the action of Chartists such as Feargus O'Connor, who wanted a more violent approach to reform. These leaders were greatly supported in many northern, industrial towns. Such an attitude alienated a government which feared civil disorder.

Thus, the three Petitions were rejected by a parliament dominated by the landed classes. As **Source A** makes clear, the Chartists failed in the short term. Even economic conditions seemed to go against them and 'opposition to the Anti-Corn Law League cut them off from a successful reforming group' trying to help the working class. **Source A** should be accurate and reliable. The author will have studied carefully to try to present an honest view of the past.

Divisions within the Chartist ranks, as men like Thomas Attwood favoured peaceful persuasion over violence, also weakened the movement, contributing to its short-term failure.

However, as **Source A** states, all was not lost. Some working-class political rights were won through the Reform Bills of 1867 and 1884, which had been influenced by the work of the Chartists. The secret ballot came in 1872, MPs were paid in 1911. Indeed, five of the six original Chartist points have been achieved. This is not a sign of failure. Chartism also helped to bring many members of the upper classes to a more sympathetic view of reform.

When seen in the short term, Chartism may be considered a failure. When looked at over several decades, the reverse is true.

Notes: _____

_____

_____

_____

_____

_____

_____

_____

_____

_____

_____

_____

_____

26 The Crimean War, 1854–56

→ Question

Using **ALL** the sources and your own knowledge, how successful was the Crimean War?

Answer

From these sources and the general background of history, it may be reasonably argued that the Crimean War was successful for Britain in the short run, but much less so in the longer term.

In 1854, Britain went to war against Russia. Russia seemed a danger to Britain's imperial interests. She posed a threat to India and seemed ready to increase her power in the Baltic. Russia had tried to make deals with Turkey in an effort to gain access to the Mediterranean. She also claimed to be the 'protector' of Slav Christians under Turkish rule. This was viewed as a threat to Turkey and as an excuse for possible Russian interference.

Britain saw all this as a potential challenge to her political, military and economic power. Although Britain, as an ally of France, supported Turkey in the war, the main British motive for fighting was self-interest and self-preservation.

Throughout the war, military successes came with victories at the battles of the Alma, Inkerman and Balaclava. But losses were heavy.

Source B describes the fighting at the battle of Inkerman. It tells of the bloody hand-to-hand struggle with bayonets, with bravery, fury and determination on both sides until 'the battalions of the Tsar gave way'.

This is useful evidence, even allowing for its bias towards the Allies. As an eyewitness account, reported for American newspaper readers, it should contain accurate details of the battle. The writer would wish to give his readers a real flavour of the event. The method of fighting suggests heavy losses on both sides. Indeed, Allied casualties amounted to 3,500 men in a costly victory.

Source C, as a painting of that famous military disaster the Charge of the Light Brigade, is probably not accurate in every detail. Nonetheless, it gives a vivid impression of a true event which was yet another costly episode of the war. Some 673 men made the charge and only about 195 returned. After reaching the Russian guns, the survivors could only retreat. This was hardly a military success, although the battle as a whole counts as a victory.

However, by 1856 the new Tsar, Alexander II, wanted peace and the war was ended by the Treaty of Paris.

The Treaty is discussed in **Source A** which, as work based on careful research and study by a modern writer, should be both reliable and accurate. **Source A** describes some of the short-term successes for Britain. Russian power and influence were cut in the Dardanelles, the Black Sea and in the Balkans. It thus appeared that Britain had had a successful war in the Crimea. Perhaps the huge death toll had been worth it? There must have been a sense of relief that Russian expansion appeared to have been checked.

Yet **Source A** also relates that by 1870 Russia felt no longer bound by the Treaty of Paris. So the Crimean War had not offered any permanent settlement of the Eastern Question. Russian power was expanding again. The war seemed to have been a wasted effort with little long-term benefit to Britain despite a short-term break from the growth of Russian power.

Notes: _____

_____

_____

_____

_____

_____

_____

_____

_____

_____

_____

_____

_____

27 The Indian Mutiny, 1857

→ Question

....

Using **ALL** the sources and your own knowledge, how far do you agree that
the Indian Mutiny doomed British control of India?

Answer

The Indian Mutiny of 1857 shocked Britain. It could have been a disaster, but
it never became a full-scale war of independence. It was quickly crushed and
British control remained firm.

The Mutiny began when Sepoys at Meerut and Delhi turned against their
British officers. Sepoy regiments in the north-west province followed suit.
One cause was a rumour that Lee Enfield cartridges were greased with pig and
cow fat. As the end of the cartridge had to be bitten off, this offended both
Muslims and Hindus.

Rebellion was also sparked by hatred of the East India Company with
its military and economic grip on the country. Lord Dalhousie's policy of
Westernisation and the seizure of territories under the Doctrine of Lapse led
to further Anglo-Indian tension.

Passions aroused by hatred of the British and, in turn, the need for Britain
to reassert herself after the Mutiny led to atrocities on both sides, as shown
in **Sources A** and **C**.

Source A describes the massacre of the men and more than 200 women
and children by the troops of Nana Sahib after receiving the British surrender
at Cawnpore. Despite the fact that this is a British source, which may show
the Indian rebels in the cruellest way, it is probably accurate. Brutality was
common in the mutiny and **Source A** was published soon after the events it
recounts. It is a useful source of information.

So also is **Source C**. This again is British evidence from soon after the
mutiny. Although not accurate in all its details, the picture is useful in
showing harsh British actions in an attempt to re-establish authority quickly.
Perhaps the British were so cruel in retaliation for what their own troops and
civilians had suffered?

It is true to say that the mutiny led to some changes as mentioned in
Source B. The role of the East India Company altered. India received a viceroy
responsible to the British government. Indians had greater responsibility in
the army and the civilian administration. As the work of a modern historian,
Source B should be accurate, reliable and objective, as the writer tries to
produce a truthful analysis. After the mutiny, Indians were allowed, for the
first time, to take part in the justice system.

But the mutiny never doomed British control. In military terms, it was a
small-scale affair. Only in the Bengal Army were there revolts but with no
more than 25 per cent of the Sepoys taking part. The mutineers were badly
organised and directed despite some brave, individual leaders. True, had the
mutiny spread, the British position would have been weak, with only about
40,000 European troops in India. But it did not.

In 1876, Queen Victoria was declared Empress of India symbolising a firm
British grip on the country. India remained a key part of the British Empire.
Britain continued to regard it as her destiny to rule a country which, she

believed, would fall apart without her unifying control owing to the many different cultures, languages and religions.

Nothing seemed to shake British control and Indian soldiers faithfully served Britain in the two World Wars. Indian independence came eventually in 1947. At the time of the Indian Mutiny, the work of leaders like Gandhi was in the distant future. Perhaps the very struggles he endured demonstrate that British control was not doomed by the Indian Mutiny?

Notes: _____

_____

_____

_____

_____

_____

_____

_____

_____

_____

_____

_____

_____

Slavery

→ Question

Using **ALL** the sources and your own knowledge, how far do you agree that the slave trade benefited Britain?

Answer

There is no doubt that Britain benefited from the slave trade, which flourished particularly in the second half of the eighteenth century until its formal abolition within the British Empire in 1833.

That it prospered was due in part to the fact that contemporaries regarded it as perfectly normal. Slavery was simply part of an economic pattern. There were few political, legal or religious objections, as noted in **Source A**. Many groups in British society had profitable vested interests in the system.

First came the trading companies, individual traders and captains. Huge profits could be made by taking slaves from Africa to work in the West Indian sugar and tobacco plantations. As the sale of every slave meant profit for the company, captain or trader, maximum numbers were crammed onto slave ships. It was important to ensure that there were enough slaves aboard to make a profit in the event of deaths during the voyage.

Sources B and **C** reflect this practice. **Source B** is an eyewitness account and the plain, factual style of the narrative suggests that what the author describes was true. **Source B** provides reliable and useful evidence concerning conditions on slave ships.

So, too, does **Source C**. This looks like an official plan of a British slave ship. As such, it will be accurate. It illustrates how the ship was filled, crammed to capacity, leading to those conditions described in **Source B**.

Another vested interest lay with those running the slave ports such as Bristol and Liverpool. Fine architecture in parts of these cities testifies to the huge benefits to those dealing in human cargoes.

The slave trade also brought great financial benefits to merchants. Extensive economic gains could be had by swapping cloth, weapons and many other manufactured goods for human beings transported to the Caribbean. Then the merchants carried home valuable supplies of sugar, tobacco and rum.

Slavery also benefited Britain as an element of her growing commercial empire, allowing it to flourish and generate great financial profits as well as increased political and military power.

Source A speaks of the high proportion of slaves serving British business interests: about 41 per cent according to the figures mentioned in the source. British commerce was expanding rapidly and the demand for slave labour was high. As **Source A** notes, the slave trade was seen as 'a pillar of the plantations', especially the sugar colonies.

The evidence of **Source A** ought to be accurate and reliable as the work of a modern historian trying to present the truth. It certainly offers useful material for considering Britain's use of slaves and contemporary attitudes to slavery.

The slave trade also benefited Britain by strengthening the developing global patterns of trade which, in turn, led to an increase in Britain's wealth.

Until abolitionists such as Clarkson and Wilberforce began their campaign against slavery, any concern for human misery was sacrificed to economic gain; only profit mattered. The abolitionists eventually won through, but it was a struggle to change a mindset favouring a system from which so many gained so much. Despite its inhuman practices, the slave trade benefited Britain greatly.

Notes: _____

_____

_____

_____

_____

_____

_____

_____

_____

_____

_____

_____

_____

Public health

→ Question

Question

Using **ALL** the sources and your own knowledge, how far is it true that major improvements to public health in the 1800s were achieved mainly through the work of individuals rather than official authorities?

Answer

The work of individuals was important for the improvement of public health during the 1800s. Their significance often lay in stirring official authorities into action. However, improvement came from a variety of other factors as well.

Source A describes Edwin Chadwick's importance. His detailed Reports of 1842 and 1844 clearly had an impact on government, leading to many improvements in drainage, sewage and general sanitation.

Source B supports **Source A** over these issues being major health concerns. Chadwick evidently identified a number of factors like overcrowded houses, filth and poor sanitation as health hazards needing treatment.

Both sources are accurate and reliable and therefore useful for an understanding of some of the public health issues of the day. **Source A** gives material from a modern historian, presented after careful reading and study. **Source B** is a factual report packed with data. It is perhaps biased as Chadwick is making his case strongly, hoping for government action. Nonetheless, the description seems balanced. Certainly **Source B** is useful in showing Chadwick's opinion of the causes of 'various forms of epidemics, and other diseases' and the required remedies.

But Chadwick's work might have fallen on deaf ears. Without action by 'official authorities' like central and local government, public health improvements would have been limited.

However, the government responded. Many improvements were carried out through the Public Health Acts of 1848, 1858 and 1875. By these, issues such as poor sanitation, water quality, sewage and drainage were tackled. Housing, too, was improved through the Artisans Dwellings Act (1875), allowing local authorities to buy up and renovate sub-standard housing.

Source C illustrates London's positive response to pressure for better sewers. The Fleet Sewer and the whole of London's sewage network represent a great feat of engineering as well as the determination of an 'official' authority to improve public health. Indeed, this commitment seems strengthened by London's further extension of her sewers.

Other factors, too, helped to drive forward public health improvements. The cholera outbreaks of 1831, 1848, 1854 and 1865 spurred on investigations into the causes of the disease and public health benefited from the research of John Snow.

Public health was also promoted by improvements in medicine and doctors. Joseph Lister pioneered antiseptic surgery. Henry Acland reformed medical training at Oxford and doctors became regulated by the British Medical Association after 1858.

The long-term influence of Florence Nightingale transformed the nursing profession after the establishment of her School of Nursing at St Thomas's Hospital, London, in 1860. Even medical technology improved with the development of the clinical thermometer, the syringe and the stethoscope. Better biology led to a greater understanding of diseases and their causes. More hospitals were created, resulting in a national network of infirmaries and hospitals by the 1890s.

During the 1800s, improvements in public health were notable. In these, individuals played a key role. However, they were helped by 'official authorities' and a range of other influences connected with neither.

Notes: _____

_____

_____

_____

_____

_____

_____

_____

_____

_____

_____

_____

_____

The Suffragettes

→ Question

Using **ALL** the sources and your own knowledge, do you think it is true to say that the militant tactics of the Suffragettes did more harm than good to their cause?

Answer

In June 1918, the Representation of the People Act granted the vote to 8.4 million women aged 30 and over. But women did not win the vote through militancy, which conversely proved harmful to their cause.

The foundress of the Suffragette Movement, Emmeline Pankhurst, and her daughters, Christabel and Sylvia, saw the use of militancy as being fully justified because the campaign for female suffrage had so far been fruitless. Thus the Pankhursts tried to mobilise public opposition to the government through the use of militant tactics.

Militancy is described in all three sources. **Source A** mentions attacks on policemen, women chaining themselves to railings and the slashing of a picture in the National Gallery. This refers to Mary Richardson, who in 1914 damaged the *Rokeby Venus*. A year earlier, Emily Davison made history by throwing herself under the King's horse in the Epsom Derby and dying from her injuries.

Militancy took many forms. Government ministers were threatened, political meetings were disrupted and pillar boxes were burnt. Arrested Suffragettes went on hunger strike in prison and were force fed. To avoid deaths, and thereby Suffragette martyrs, the government passed the Cat-and-Mouse Act in 1913. This allowed the release of sick protesters but their re-arrest when they were better. **Source B** tells of an unsuccessful bomb threat at St Paul's and in **Source C**, Suffragettes are seen smashing windows.

All three sources are useful and reliable. The information in **Source A** is the balanced analysis of a modern historian after careful study. That in **Source B**, although under a headline suggesting disgust, gives a clear account of what had taken place. Although the details of the illustration in **Source C** are probably not accurate, it depicts, nonetheless, true happenings. Indeed, both **Sources B** and **C** furnish much useful contemporary information.

But the militant Suffragettes were unable to harness the support of either the Labour movement or of working-class women. They thus failed to create a genuine mass women's movement, allowing the government to act freely against them.

In the end, militancy became harmful to their objectives. Suffragette violence and disregard for law and order disgusted many. Increasing numbers of women disassociated themselves from the movement by joining non-militant groups. Militant tactics antagonised pro-Suffragette MPs and the very people in government with the power to grant them their demands. Such a fierce approach shook their cause badly in the short term.

The Suffragettes were perhaps saved by the outbreak of war in 1914. Imprisoned militants were released and, as noted in **Source A**, 'the Suffragette campaign was halted'. Violence was suspended. Mrs Pankhurst and Christabel now used their energies to support the government. They encouraged recruiting and discouraged workers from damaging the war effort through strikes.

Women then played a vital role on the Home Front. They nursed, drove buses and delivered post. They worked in munitions and engineering factories and on farms. Many even demanded equal pay! By 1918, women had showed themselves worthy of the vote and they got it; not through militancy which had damaged their cause, but through honest and constructive effort.

Notes: _____

_____

_____

_____

_____

_____

_____

_____

_____

_____

_____

_____

ANSWERS TO SAMPLE ESSAY QUESTIONS 1066–1914

Answers to essay questions

Here are three attempts to answer this question, which reflect the different standards of answer as described in the ISEB mark scheme (see page 86). Pay particular attention to those at **Level 3**. This is the standard you are aiming for: the others are there to show you what **not** to do!

→ Question

From the period you have studied choose any one important political event and explain its importance.

Level 3 answer: The sealing of Magna Carta, 1215

At Runnymede in June 1215, King John was faced by his barons and sealed an important document known as Magna Carta. John had failed in war, losing Normandy in 1204. He had fallen out with Pope Innocent III and the result was that, for a time, England was put under Interdict and surrendered as a Papal Fief. The barons thought that John had abused unwritten feudal customs by raising taxes himself and taking rights such as scutage when there was no war. All this angered them and led them to take action against the king. The result was Magna Carta or The Great Charter.

This Charter is important in many ways. The fact that John was forced to agree to it shows that monarchs could be controlled by the actions of a powerful baronage. In 1215, John was ordered to rule according to the customs of the kingdom and a committee of 25 barons was appointed to keep a check on him.

The appearance of Magna Carta meant that future kings, too, had to observe their side of feudal law and not try to abuse their royal powers. Although the Charter was produced in response to the immediate problems of the years leading up to 1215, it set a pattern for the future. This was important for the cause of Baronial Reform. If any king tried to take too much power again, the nobles had an example to follow. Indeed, the Charter was constantly referred to in the various disputes between the barons and Henry III right up to 1272 and beyond.

Magna Carta was also notable as it shows that the barons were keen to protect themselves against any reduction of their feudal rights.

Another significant point about Magna Carta was that it laid down the standards to be observed by kings. It also provided the first written definition of royal rights. It thus played a vital part in establishing the limits of royal power and shaping the role of monarchs in their running of the country. The Charter guided them towards a working political partnership with their nobles and, later, with their parliaments.

Through the Charter, basic rights concerning taxation and freedom had been raised, discussed (or argued over) and then written down, which was an important part of establishing what these rights actually were.

Two further points about the Great Charter deserve attention owing to their importance. Firstly, John promised to respect the rights of the Church. He had been taking Church money illegally and interfering with Church privileges. After Magna Carta, the liberties and revenues of the Church were respected and protected and many royal abuses were ended. Secondly, John promised not to sell or refuse justice. Freemen could no longer be punished or imprisoned without a fair trial by their peers (equals). This established some key principles of law which still apply today and thus stresses the long-term importance of 1215.

Such rights would gradually filter down to ordinary people in the course of time. Thus the Charter's importance is not restricted to kings and noblemen; all classes gained from it eventually.

In conclusion, it may be seen that the sealing of Magna Carta was an important political event. However, its effects extended also to economic, social and religious matters. Its overall impact is not just restricted to 1215 or to the short term. Indeed, such is the significance of the Charter that some of its chapters still remain on the Statute Book. The spirit of the Charter lives on.

These long-term consequences are a vital element of the significance of what took place that June day on that little island in the River Thames. When added to the short-term consequences, they show just how important Magna Carta was, and is.

Comments related to mark scheme

- This is a well-structured essay with a clear introduction and conclusion which sandwich a precise framework of argument and analysis.

- The opening narrative sets the scene. It leads nicely into the main body of the essay. This is the function of an introduction (from the Latin *intro* – I enter and *duco* – I lead). The reader is 'led into' the essay.

- The opening factual comments serve to establish the reader's confidence in you, the writer.

- All knowledge is relevant to the question. It is precisely selected.

- Comments and assertions are supported by facts where necessary.

- The significance of the material is constantly stressed. In an essay concerning the importance of something, this is vital.

- Both the short-term and the long-term importance of Magna Carta are considered. This is a useful way to group consequences.

- Specialist words like, 'feudal', and 'scutage' are appropriately used. If you are studying this period and this topic in particular, you should know these terms.

- The conclusion refers relevantly to the essay title and offers some sensible general comments, as well as making a final judgement.

Level 2 answer: The sealing of Magna Carta, 1215

Magna Carta is the name given to the Great Charter which was sealed by King John at Runnymede, on the banks of the Thames near Windsor in June 1215. It is a very important document.

John had been a very bad king since he had come to the throne in 1199. During his reign, lots of things went wrong and the barons became increasingly angry. So they decided to make a charter. This is one of the reasons why Magna Carta is important; it shows an attempt by the nobility to control their king.

There were many causes of the revolt of the barons against King John. They were upset at his failures in foreign policy, especially at the loss of Normandy in 1204.

The barons also objected to John's abuse of his feudal powers. He had been overcharging for reliefs (payments to a lord when a tenant took over his land) and had taken scutage when there was no war. John had also personally raised high taxes. He had interfered with the law, which meant much corruption and unfair treatment in the courts.

John refused to meet his barons. This led them to raise an army and force him to agree to Magna Carta. Archbishop Stephen Langton helped to get the two sides together.

The Charter stated that John was to respect the rights of the Church. This was an important matter. John was not allowed to raise taxes without the approval of his noblemen. The barons took much more control over feudal matters like scutage and reliefs.

A very important part of the Charter was to do with justice. No freeman could be imprisoned or punished without a trial by his peers. This became a notable point of law and meant better and fairer justice for more people. John was also banned from selling justice, which he had been doing, so the law was improved and made fairer. This is another important result of the Charter.

The barons were keen to protect themselves and this was one of the main reasons they demanded a charter in 1215. John now had to keep to all the proper customs of England. A committee of 25 barons was set up to watch over him and to make sure that he did what he was told.

Magna Carta came about because of the immediate feudal problems of the early 1200s. The truth of this can be seen in many of the things it said. Magna Carta also laid down the rules for being a king, which monarchs after John would have to follow. Also, the rights and powers of a king were written down for the first time.

At the start Magna Carta, and the good things it brought for the Church and the law, was mainly limited to the king and the upper classes. However, in time, some of the benefits helped the lower classes. For instance, a lower-class man was now more likely to get fairer treatment in a court of law.

Some of the things that the Charter did are still important today. It has been said that when Magna Carta was made, it was a moment when the rights of the English people were strengthened.

Comments related to mark scheme

- No initial thesis or relevant introduction.

- Some extended and accurate narrative, but much is undirected to the specific demands of the question.

- Too much material skirts around the question without answering it.

- Occasional reference to the question.

- Too much *implied* importance. The case for the importance of Magna Carta is not made directly enough.

- Some failure to comment on the significance of the material in relation to the question.

- Occasional attempts at relevant arguments, but much is undeveloped.

- Justification of some statements, but largely undeveloped.

- Occasional realisation of the significance of what is said.

- Uncertain structure overall.

- Conclusion is too short despite making one valid point.

- In general, the reader feels that the question was not answered fully or relevantly despite the writer's knowledge and understanding of some of the issues. Better use could have been made of this knowledge and understanding through a greater sense of relevance.

Level 1 answer: The sealing of Magna Carta, 1215

Magna Carta is important. King John had come to the throne in 1199. He was a very bad king who managed to lose the Crown Jewels in the Wash and died from eating too many peaches and drinking cider. At the end of his journey, John was too ill to ride and had to be carried in a litter. He died at Newark and was buried in a cathedral near to the shrine of his favourite saint.

Magna Carta was a charter made in 1215. It was signed by John and his barons. It had lots of parts to it and the barons made John sign it because they wanted more power.

Magna Carta was all to do with the feudal system. John had lots of power given to him because he was the king at the top. But John did much that was wrong. He did horrid things to the Church so that the bishops and priests did not like him very much.

In the law, John made the judges do as he said. He was not very honest in the law. Some people were not allowed to go to court, while others did not get a fair trial. Some were put in prison wrongly and widows had to give the king lots of money.

John also murdered his friend, Arthur, so that he could get lots of power and be safe as king.

John did lots of things in his foreign policy. He did not like the king of France, so he went to war against him. The war did not go very well. John lost lots of battles and land. This was because the English soldiers were not very good and the French were better. This is why John took lots of money from many people. He needed cash to pay for his wars.

Because of this, John's barons were unhappy and did not like him. Neither did all the people in the Church and the law. Because many people did not like him, Magna Carta was invented and John had to sign it. Some people say that John did not actually sign the Charter, but sealed it. Whatever he did, the Charter was an important document. The signing, or sealing, on an island in the River Thames, was an important political event as the question says.

About 40 copies of the Charter were made. It was all written in Latin and not many copies are left now. There is one in London and another in the cathedral at Salisbury.

Some of the Charter said that John should leave the Church alone. He was not allowed to raise any new taxes or to take any more money from people without his barons letting him. Everybody was to have a fair trial and they could not be put in prison without going to court. All punishments had to match the crime.

There are over 60 paragraphs in the Charter. It is a long document, which is a reason why it is important. Another reason for its importance is because it is kind to widows. One bit of the Charter says, 'No widow shall be forced to marry so long as she wishes to live without a husband'.

Magna Carta is an important document for all these reasons.

Comments related to mark scheme

- Read this carefully to see what **not** to do!

- No introduction to set the scene.

- A conclusion which, although true, does not follow on from the essay.

- Much vague knowledge; a lack of detail in parts.

- Some accurate and precise knowledge, but largely unrelated to the question and not helping to show the *importance* of Magna Carta.

- There is some general knowledge and the quotation of Clause 8, concerning widows (obviously learnt) at the end, comes as a surprise. The surrounding sentences suggest that it is perhaps not fully understood.

- Little precise selection of relevant knowledge. Topic knowledge is tangled up with question knowledge.

- No judgement or precise evaluation of the material.

- No clear or consistent argument throughout.

- Some understanding that Magna Carta is an important document, but no full explanation or justification of this opinion.

Notes: _____

_____

_____

_____

_____

_____

_____

_____

_____

_____

_____

Here are three attempts to answer this question, which reflect the different standards of answer as described in the ISEB mark scheme (see page 86). Pay particular attention to those at **Level 3**. This is the standard you are aiming for: the others are there to show you what **not** to do!

→ Question

Explain the consequences of any one war you have studied.

Level 3 answer: The consequences of the War of the Spanish Succession 1702–13

During the final decades of the seventeenth century, the European scene was dominated by the attempts of Louis XIV to extend the power of France. This worried both the Dutch and the German Emperor. Matters came to a head over the Spanish succession in 1700, after the death of Charles II. Louis had cleverly managed to get his grandson, Philip, Duke of Anjou, onto the Spanish throne. This meant a great increase in French power and a complete upset of the balance of power in favour of France. So, in 1702, England went to war to challenge this. Overall, the conflict was a triumph for England and with the Treaty of Utrecht (1713) came a series of notable consequences for England, both in the long and short term.

In political terms, victory in 1713 strengthened both Queen Anne and her government. It also meant a general increase in the power and prestige of England abroad. Other countries now saw England in a new light and treated her with more respect as the idea of French invincibility was shattered. English international power was firmly established. This was shown in the longer term through important gains of territory in the treaties such as the Peace of Paris (1763). These partly followed on from Utrecht.

In military and diplomatic terms, too, the War of the Spanish Succession represented a triumphal outcome for England. In 1713, England gained Gibraltar, Minorca, Newfoundland and Nova Scotia. This increased her military and political power in North America and the Mediterranean both in the short term and in the decades to come. The gaining of such lands formed part of the steady growth of what was to become the British Empire.

This expansion of Empire led to important economic consequences. After the Treaty of Utrecht, England was able to establish trading links with her new lands and so establish global patterns of trade. This served to increase her wealth further, as well as to sustain more political and military power. It also helped to provide extensive markets for commercial goods, as production gradually increased throughout the 1700s and on into the next century. The Treaty of Utrecht was a pivotal point in all of this; it encouraged economic growth.

In religious matters, too, the War of the Spanish Succession brought benefits. In the short term Louis XIV promised to recognise the Protestant Succession in England. Despite the Jacobite Rebellions of 1715 and 1745, the Protestant Hanoverians were able to maintain and strengthen their religious position throughout the rest of the century.

It might even be argued that the War of the Spanish Succession had important cultural consequences for England. In February 1705, the Duke of Marlborough (one of England's most successful military commanders in the war) was granted a royal estate at Woodstock as a reward for his great victory at the Battle of Blenheim. Over the next twenty years, there grew up a splendid Baroque palace. This was designed and built by famous architects like Vanbrugh and Hawksmoor and decorated by top craftsmen such as Grinling Gibbons and Louis Laguerre. In the 1760s, Capability Brown developed the landscape with its great lake. Blenheim Palace is now an important part of England's heritage and a World Heritage Site. Perhaps it would not have been built had it not been for the War of the Spanish Succession?

There is no doubt that the War of the Spanish Succession had great consequences for England. The Protestant Succession was saved. The Empire was extended and naval supremacy was established in the Mediterranean. There was a new European balance of power in which England came to play a leading part, eventually extending her influence around the globe. Despite the great debts created through running the war, the conflict had brought important political, military, economic, religious and cultural gains.

Comments related to mark scheme
- Good, strong introduction which sets the scene.

- Well-structured central section.

- Strong and relevant conclusion.

- Relevant writing throughout.

- Precise selection of material in relation to the question.

- Thematic treatment of the material (political, military, diplomatic, religious, cultural); this helps generate good structure and avoids narrative.

- Consideration of the consequences over time: short-term, long-term results. This again promotes good structure.

- Consequences are evaluated within their context.

- No narrative slabs.

- Sensible judgements.

- Assertions and comments are fully justified.

Level 2 answer: The consequences of the War of the Spanish Succession 1702–13

The War of the Spanish Succession started in 1702. Louis XIV of France had been following an aggressive foreign policy in Europe. He had threatened the Dutch in the 1670s. During the 1690s he attacked them again. He also began to threaten the German Empire.

By 1700, Spain, although still having a large empire, was weak and in decline. Both the Hapsburgs and the Bourbons were interested in getting some territory as the dying king, Charles II, had no heir.

Some partition treaties had been made to divide land between the various candidates. However, Louis XIV had been active in secret and in 1700, when Charles II died, Louis made sure that the whole of the Spanish Empire was inherited by his grandson Philip, Duke of Anjou. He took over as Philip V of Spain. Louis was pleased, but England, the Dutch and the German Emperor were not happy. Louis had upset the European balance of power and had tilted it firmly towards France.

England thus went to war to restore the balance of power and to prevent any union between France and Spain.

The Duke of Marlborough was made Commander-in-Chief of the Allied forces. He was a brilliant soldier. He decided to march down the Rhine to meet his ally, Eugene of Savoy, and crush the Elector of Bavaria, who was threatening Vienna, the imperial capital. This march was a great military achievement. Marlborough supplied more than 40,000 soldiers and 14,000 cavalry in the long march to the Danube.

In August 1704, Marlborough and Eugene met the French army, commanded by Marshal Tallard, at Blenheim. A bloody battle followed. It was an allied victory. Tallard was captured and the French were driven from the battlefield with great losses.

Marlborough wrote a famous note to Sarah, his wife. This is called the Blenheim Dispatch. It said, 'I have not time to say more, but beg you will give my duty to the queen, and let her know her army has had a glorious victory'. More than 20,000 Frenchmen were killed and Marlborough took over 14,000 prisoners.

Marlborough then had more great victories. These were: Ramillies (1706), Oudenarde (1708) and Malplaquet (1709). By this time, Louis XIV wanted peace, so the Treaty of Utrecht was made in 1713. This ended the war. France had been defeated.

There were lots of consequences for England. Firstly, she gained lands such as Nova Scotia and Newfoundland. France was forced to accept the Protestant Succession. This made Queen Anne stronger and also the Hanoverian kings who came after her. They were all Protestant.

Because England had won the war, she was seen as a great power and an important influence. After 1713, England was treated with much more respect by the other countries.

Now that England had gained more lands, she was able to increase her trade. This meant she was richer and stronger because countries that have lots of money are usually powerful.

In conclusion, it is fair to say that the consequences of the War of the Spanish Succession were very good for England and for Queen Anne and her government.

Comments related to mark scheme

- The key problem here is that the essay only starts to answer the question in the final four paragraphs. The writer has left it far too late to start being relevant. This is a common fault often seen in exam scripts. Get going on the question straight away!

- There is a large slab of narrative, often accurate, but unrelated to the demands of the question.

- There is no introduction. The story just begins.

- The structure of the piece is not suited to the production of a relevant answer. It is shaped by the idea of narrative. Any mention or analysis of the consequences of the war is thus naturally pushed towards the end of the answer.

- There is some substantiation of assertions, but it is undeveloped.

- The conclusion is accurate, but based only on the final paragraphs.

- There is much wasted knowledge here. Material has not been selected in relation to the question.

Level 1 answer: The consequences of the War of the Spanish Succession 1702–13

In 1702, England went to war against France. The king of France was Louis XIV and he had been trying to get too much power in Europe. There was a balance of power in Europe and Louis was trying to upset it. He had been attacking the Dutch who managed to hold him off. He had also been trying to get some power over the German Emperor.

In 1700, the king of Spain died and there was no one to take his place. Louis XIV got his grandson Philip made Philip V of Spain. This made France very powerful. Louis XIV, who lived at Versailles, now had control over both France and Spain. All the other countries did not like this. They ganged up on Louis and so war came.

On England's side were the Dutch, the German Emperor and some German princes. On the French side were some German princes as well.

The French army was led by Marshal Tallard. The English army was led by the Duke of Marlborough. He was a very great soldier and because of him, England won the war and there were some very important consequences.

Marlborough made a long march down the Rhine. This was called 'the red caterpillar' by Winston Churchill because all the English soldiers had red uniforms. So as they marched along in a line, they looked a bit like a caterpillar.

When they got to Blenheim they met Prince Eugene who was on our side. Then a big battle took place. Lots of soldiers on both sides were killed, but England won and Marlborough was a hero.

Because of this, Marlborough was given Blenheim Palace as a present from Queen Anne. Marlborough went on to win lots of other battles. One of them was the Battle of Malplaquet. In the end because of all Marlborough's great victories, England won the war.

A peace agreement was made in 1713. By this, England gained lots of things. England got new lands like Nova Scotia and Gibraltar. This was important. Gibraltar was a good naval base and still is today. By getting Gibraltar England had a proper place to put some of her fleet. This was good because having lots of ports was useful at that time when ships could not sail very far and had to keep stopping at places to get fresh food and water.

The Queen and the British government were pleased that we won the War of the Spanish Succession because that made us a strong country. It meant we could have lots of power and rule over the other countries.

Having many new lands by winning the war meant that England could start her Empire. This was another good result of Marlborough's victories. Marlborough is one of England's greatest heroes. After he had won the battle at Blenheim, one consequence was that he wrote a letter to his wife on the back of a pub bill. This showed that he had bought some bread and meat.

England did well to win the War of the Spanish Succession. It was mainly because of Marlborough being such a great soldier. He brought lots of consequences for his country.

Comments related to mark scheme
- A general ramble here. No attempt to plan a structured or relevant answer. A stream of factual material with little comment is offered. Much is off the point and some is inaccurate.

- No introduction to set the scene.

- Vague knowledge in too many places.

- Poor style, including simple statements often without any justification.

- Little evaluation of the material.

- Much is undeveloped; for example, the idea that Gibraltar is an important military base.

- There are too many irrelevant asides. These add nothing to the answer. In an exam, they merely waste time.

- There is a hint of misunderstanding of the word consequences, and of the question in general.

Here are three attempts to answer this question, which reflect the different standards of answer as described in the ISEB mark scheme (see page 86). Pay particular attention to those at **Level 3**. This is the standard you are aiming for: the others are there to show you what **not** to do!

→ Question

Explain the importance of the work of any one government minister in the period you have studied.

Level 3 answer: The importance of the work of Robert Peel as prime minister, 1841–46

Robert Peel, Prime Minister 1841–46, was in power at a time of great reform in Britain. His most significant work concerned domestic matters. The Industrial Revolution was transforming the country, creating both a powerful, wealthy middle class and an industrial workforce, often living in squalid conditions. Perhaps the overall importance of Peel's work was that he saw the need for change and acted upon his observations.

Peel, as a Tory, was a cautious reformer. He championed the idea of slow evolution rather than revolution overnight. His careful reforms ensured that Britain underwent change gradually, rather than facing the violence apparent in many other European countries at this time.

In 1841, Peel clearly saw some of Britain's problems. There was a trade slump and bad working conditions in many factories. A series of poor harvests made life hard for all, but especially the poor. In the north of England, there was much unemployment and unrest in many cotton towns such as Manchester.

In economic matters, Peel's reforms did much to improve the lives of many. Peel said that he wanted to make this country 'a cheap place for living'. He supported the idea of free trade both to reduce the cost of living and to stimulate international commerce.

In his budget of 1842, he reduced duties on over 750 articles. Further such reductions followed in 1844, 1845 and 1846. Indeed, by 1846, more than 75 per cent of those duties existing in 1841 had been scrapped. These changes were important in that they eased the lives of many poorer people as some goods became cheaper.

With this reduction in duties, Peel had to obtain money from elsewhere. He thus took a sensible and important (if unpopular) decision to tax those people who could pay. So, income tax at a rate of 7d in the pound (about 2.9 per cent) was introduced on all incomes over £150 a year. The success of these measures was significant and the government was £2 million in credit by 1844.

Peel's ministry was also important in social terms. Laws such as the Mines Act of 1842, which stopped women and girls, and boys under ten from working underground, and the 1844 Factory Act, did much to improve the working conditions of the labouring classes.

Much of this reform was opposed by both Whigs and Tories who resented increased government interference. Peel's importance in this work lies in the fact that he had the drive, determination and administrative ability to force changes through, to the benefit of many.

Peel's most important political achievement, which had many economic and social consequences, was his repeal of the Corn Laws in 1846. All duties on wheat, oats and barley were abolished. This act eventually brought Peel down, but there was no disaster for agriculture or for the landowning classes as had been feared by some. Peel's work here strengthened the important idea that his government was committed to reform. In this case he could argue that the Corn Laws had been sacrificed to feed the people.

Robert Peel's work was important for many reasons. His measures strengthened the cause of reform. Peel's actions showed him as a visionary who saw the need for reform and took a practical approach to it. His policies are also significant as they demonstrate that he was a man who was not afraid to put principle before popularity, even though it cost him his job as prime minister.

Comments related to mark scheme

● There is a good, clear introduction which sets the scene and prepares the reader for what follows.

● Topic knowledge has been precisely selected to be relevant and to match the needs of the question.

● There is strong analysis throughout.

● Factual material is accurate. It is there only to underpin assertions and not for its own sake.

● All the material is discussed and analysed in relation to *importance*, which is the key subject of the question.

● There are clear arguments and balanced judgements.

● The material has been arranged thematically (social, economic). This is a useful way to avoid mere narrative and to generate relevance.

● There is a strong conclusion with sensible general statements.

Level 2 answer: The importance of the work of Robert Peel as prime minister, 1841–46

When Robert Peel became prime minister in 1841, he had a modern outlook and saw that there was a need for reform in many areas of British life. This was an important factor in the direction of his work.

Peel wanted to make Britain a cheap place to live in. This was an important idea for all classes of people, especially the factory workers and the unemployed. Peel supported the idea of free trade to reduce living costs and to stimulate commerce.

Peel's budgets of 1842, 1844, 1845 and 1846 abolished many import and export duties. He stabilised the economy through the Bank Charter Act (1844). He introduced Income Tax at 7d in the pound (2.9 per cent) on salaries of more than £150 a year. Peel's financial policies were successful and, by 1844, government income was more than it spent by about £2 million. This was a significant achievement by Peel.

Robert Peel supported Shaftesbury in his social reforms. The Mines Act (1842) introduced limited inspections of pits and stopped women, girls, and boys under ten from working underground. The Factory Act of 1844 helped the workers by limiting the number of daily workable hours.

Many of these reforms were opposed by both Whigs and Tories. They said that they would lead to a fall in output. Increasing government interference was also resented.

In 1841, Daniel O'Connell demanded the repeal of the Anglo-Irish Union. Two years later, Peel set up a commission to look at the Irish land problem, but the main difficulties in Ireland remained. Nonetheless, this was an important move by Peel. It at least showed that he was aware of the problem and had tried to do something about it.

In June 1846, Peel repealed the Corn Laws. The duties on wheat, barley and oats were abolished. The repeal of the Corn Laws together with the defeat of a Coercion Bill for Ireland increased the political opposition to Peel and in June 1846, he was forced to resign.

Peel's work was important because he had tried to make the lives of ordinary people better. Through the repeal of the Corn Laws, Peel was able to increase Britain's trade. Other countries eased their duties on British goods owing to the lifting of restrictions on corn imports. All of this was important.

The Corn Law Repeal was popular with reformers. Peel was important because he introduced a key reform at home by trying to make things better, when some other countries were undergoing revolutionary times. The Corn Law Repeal ensured that change in Britain occurred by evolution and not by revolution. It strengthened the idea that the government had sacrificed the Corn Laws to feed its people.

Peel's work is also important because it shows a man who had clear ideas and who wanted to do his best for the people of Britain. Peel was a man who was not afraid to put his principles before his popularity. He cared about his policies and their effects rather than just wanting to hang on to power for itself. Such an attitude is important in a government minister and this is what makes Peel and his work so significant.

Comments related to mark scheme
- There is a short introduction which makes one valid point, but it could be broader in scope.

- Most of the early part of the essay is plain narrative. It is accurate, but it does not address the question.

- A few assertions are made and said to be important, but analysis is undeveloped and there is often little justification of the opinions.

- There are a few attempts at assessing the importance of what is said, but far more are required to make this a Level 3 answer.

- The structure of this essay is based on the initial slab of narrative. Any analysis of the importance of Peel's work is left to the final paragraphs where it is undeveloped. Avoid this. It is a common fault in exams. Get stuck in to the question as soon as you can.

- Towards the end, the focus of the piece drifts too much towards discussion of the repeal of the Corn Laws.

- The conclusion makes some relevant points. It needs to be broader, drawing together all the threads of the essay.

- There is, occasionally, some relevant analysis, as well as an overall recognition that the question concerns the importance of Peel's work. But, overall, this piece is too narrative to merit a top grade.

Level 1 answer: The importance of the work of Robert Peel as prime minister, 1841–46

Robert Peel was born in 1788 and died in 1850. He was the son of a rich cotton manufacturer. He was educated at Harrow and Christ Church, Oxford, founded by Cardinal Wolsey, the chief minister to Henry VIII. There, he met lots of other men from the upper classes.

Peel first got into parliament for a seat in Ireland which his father had bought for him. He was good in parliament and was made Under-Secretary for War and the Colonies when aged only 21. He was able to make effective speeches in parliament. Between 1812 and 1818, he was Chief Secretary for Ireland and in 1822, he became Home Secretary. This was a very important job. Peel made some changes to the law. The most famous thing he did was to make the Metropolitan Police Force in 1829. His new policemen wore a uniform. They also carried batons. Their main base was at Scotland Yard. Their nicknames, 'bobbies' or 'Peelers', came from Robert Peel's name.

Peel was a man with modern views even though he was a Tory. In his Tamworth Manifesto, he upset many members of his own party because he supported the basic changes made in the 1832 Reform Bill.

In 1841, Peel became prime minister. He lasted until 1846 when he was made to resign after the repeal of the Corn Laws.

Peel wanted to do lots of things for Britain to make it better and help the poor people and all the factory workers. Peel said that he wanted to reduce the cost of living and make England a cheap place to live in.

In his various budgets, Peel cut import and export duties on many things. This meant that people paid less for them and so they were better off. This made Robert Peel popular.

Peel also helped to make the mines better by not allowing women and girls to work underground. Factories were in a terrible state. They were also dangerous places with all the new machinery. So Peel passed laws to make them better. One of these laws said that there were to be factory inspectors, like school inspectors, to go round and check that everything was alright. These inspectors were not liked.

In 1847, a law said that people in textile factories should work no more than ten hours a day.

A lot of people did not like his new laws. Many others, like factory bosses, hated the idea of governments checking up on what they did.

The Anti-Corn Law League was men like Richard Cobden who hated the Corn Laws. At the same time, there was a famine in Ireland when the potato crop failed. This meant that lots of people did not have enough to eat and some starved to death. Because of this, Peel ended the Corn Laws in 1846. This was another important thing he did.

Even though ending the Corn Laws was famous and a good thing for many people, it made Peel lose his job.

Comments related to mark scheme
● No introduction to set the scene.

● Opening paragraphs beginning 'XXX was born in XXX and died in XXX. He/ she was the son/daughter of XXX ...' are usually the kiss of death for an essay. Examiners dread such starts. What follows (as here) is usually a mini-life of the person with varying degrees of factual accuracy *and, in most cases, utter irrelevance to the needs of the question*. Do not do it!!

● At first the narrative is precise (if irrelevant). It then becomes vague as knowledge runs out.

● This essay is largely irrelevant. There is no obvious attempt to answer the question.

● There is little judgement or evaluation of the material.

● There are no clear arguments and there is no analysis.

- Little relevant or justifiable opinions.
- Poor structure.
- There is an awkward English style in places.
- No conclusion offering anything relevant to the question.

Notes: _____

_____

_____

_____

_____

_____

_____

_____

_____

_____

_____

_____

_____

_____

APPENDIX
ISEB MARK SCHEMES

ISEB mark schemes

→ Evidence question

UNDERSTANDING/CROSS-REFERENCING/EVALUATION/CONTEXTUALISATION		(20)
Mark	Target	Source comprehension and interpretation; cross-referencing sources; evaluation of sources for utility and contextualisation of sources with relevant own knowledge
1–10	Level 1	**Generalised answer:** offers valid but undeveloped comments without direct support from sources or own knowledge; **or** only uses either sources or own knowledge to make undeveloped comments.
11–15	Level 2	**Supported answer:** makes links between the sources, own knowledge and the question; answers at this level will show some selection and organisation of material, but may lack structure and development; an answer at the top of this level comments upon the reliability or usefulness of the sources.
16–20	Level 3	**Focused answer:** reaches a judgement by making direct use of the sources and valid statements upon the reliability or utility of the sources, as well as contextual own knowledge; well-structured answer with sound substantiation; an answer at the top of this level attempts to explore the evidence for and against the question/statement.

→ Essay question

SELECTIVE DESCRIPTION/EVALUATION/ANALYSIS		(30)
Mark	Target	Recall/selection and presentation of relevant knowledge; evaluation of factors against one another; definitions of success and failure; contextual assessment; causes and consequences
1–10	Level 1	**Simple statements:** offers some features/ideas supported by some knowledge; embryonic, inaccurate or irrelevant knowledge; lacks real coherence and structure; offers basic and largely unfocused opinion; little judgement/assessment/evaluation offered.
11–20	Level 2	**More developed statements:** gives features supported by more relevant knowledge along with more developed analysis; some substantiation of assertions; uncertain overall structure; attempts to offer reasoned judgement/assessment/evaluation in places. **NB: Up to 15 marks may be awarded for a good narrative.**
21–30	Level 3	**Selected knowledge in a clear framework of argument:** answer shows precisely selected knowledge with strong, developed analysis/assessment and cogent, balanced judgements; strong substantiation of assertions; for top of level, coherent, substantiated argument is present throughout.